Ultimate

Trading
Spaces™

EPISODE
GUIDE

Meredith® Books
Des Moines, Iowa

Trading Spaces Ultimate Episode Guide
Editor: Amy Tincher-Durik
Senior Associate Design Director: Ken Carlson
Writer: Kellie Kramer
Contributing Art Directors: Mike Bentley, Eric Groves, C.J. Schrunk: Groves
  Design Company
Copy Chief: Terri Fredrickson
Copy and Production Editor: Victoria Forlini
Editorial Operations Manager: Karen Schirm
Managers, Book Production: Pam Kvitne, Marjorie J. Schenkelberg, Rick von Holdt
Contributing Proofreaders: Sara Henderson, Gretchen Kauffman, Jeanée Ledoux
Editorial and Design Assistants: Kaye Chabot, Karen McFadden, Mary Lee Gavin

Meredith₀ Books
Editor in Chief: Linda Raglan Cunningham
Design Director: Matt Strelecki
Executive Editor, Home Decorating and Design: Denise L. Caringer

Publisher: James D. Blume
Executive Director, Marketing: Jeffrey Myers
Executive Director, New Business Development: Todd M. Davis
Executive Director, Sales: Ken Zagor
Director, Operations: George A. Susral
Director, Production: Douglas M. Johnston
Business Director: Jim Leonard

Vice President and General Manager: Douglas J. Guendel

Meredith Publishing Group
President, Publishing Group: Stephen M. Lacy
Vice President-Publishing Director: Bob Mate

Meredith Corporation
Chairman and Chief Executive Officer: William T. Kerr

In Memoriam: E. T. Meredith III (1933—2003)

Special thanks to Banyan Productions and Ross Productions.

All of us at Meredith Books are dedicated to providing you with information and
ideas to enhance your home. We welcome your comments and suggestions. Write
to us at: Meredith Books, Home Decorating and Design Editorial Department, 1716
Locust St., Des Moines, IA 50309-3023.

If you would like to purchase any of our home decorating and design, cooking,
crafts, gardening, or home improvement books, check wherever quality books are
sold. Or visit us at: meredithbooks.com

Trading Spaces Book Development Team
Kathy Davidov, Executive Producer, TLC
Roger Marmet, General Manager, TLC
Tom Farrell, Executive Producer, Banyan Productions
Sharon M. Bennett, Senior Vice President, Strategic Partnerships & Licensing
Carol LeBlanc, Vice President, Marketing & Retail Development
Erica Jacobs Green, Publishing Manager
Elizabeth Bakacs, Creative Director, Strategic Partnerships

Contents

6 Season 1

34 Making an Episode

52 The Key Swap

68 Season 2 **82** Homework Time

120 Designer Chat

196 B-Roll

Season 3

140

168 Reveals

238 Index

Introduction

In your hands, you hold a complete, chronological tour through three seasons of America's favorite decorating show. Whether you've seen all 144 episodes, or just a handful, you will relive all the moments—such as the introduction of each cast member and the removal of the first ceiling fan—that have kept fans coming back week after week. Inside this book you'll find before-and-after photographs of every room designed for *Trading Spaces,* along with all your favorite moments—including a special look at how an episode is made and highlights such as memorable Key Swaps and Reveals. So put on your smock, call your neighbors, and get ready to have some fun!

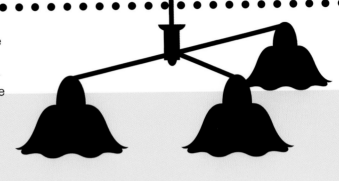

Location

Season Episode

Berkeley, CA: Prospect Street

Doug's Room: ☺ ☺ ☹   Genevieve's Room: ☺ ☺ ☹

S2

E30

👶 ⬅️📦 🎓 $ ♥

Cast: Paige, Doug, Genevieve, Ty

Smiley-Face Rating Scale

Icons

Cast

DESIGNED BY DOUG

The Rooms

Doug cleans up the Delta Upsilon fraternity chapter room (and goes DU-clectic) by painting the walls lime green, installing bench seating, constructing two huge circular ottomans upholstered with lime and orange fabrics, and suspending a tabletop from the ceiling. Gen adds classic Hollywood-style glamour to the Alpha Omicron Pi sorority chapter room by painting white and silver stripes on the walls, adding black and silver throw pillows, building a large armoire, and ...ioning her team to trace ...and herself for

...: the start of the show.

after

4

Icon Legend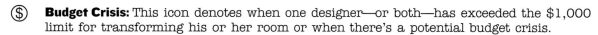

$\textcircled{\$}$ **Budget Crisis:** This icon denotes when one designer—or both—has exceeded the $1,000 limit for transforming his or her room or when there's a potential budget crisis.

Carpenter to the Rescue: Whether it's Amy Wynn refiguring a measurement or Ty developing a plan to save money on lumber, the carpenters get due credit for their problem-solving abilities.

Ceiling Fan: Most often this icon points out when a ceiling fan has been removed from a room, but sometimes a fan has been added—or the existing fan altered—to better suit the newly transformed room.

Celebrity Episode: Even famous actors, musicians, and personalities have partaken in the fun of *Trading Spaces*!

College Episode: In these episodes, there's no cramming for finals or secret handshakes to remember, but there's plenty of campus comedy.

Demolition: Whenever this icon appears, rest assured that sledgehammers—and sometimes bare hands—are dismantling something.

♥ **Fan Favorite:** Whether they feature a project that didn't quite work out, debates between cast members and homeowners, great room designs, or memorable Reveals, these are the episodes people talk about—long after an episode has aired!

Paint Extravaganza: An extravaganza of color, that is! This icon begs the question, why paint a room with one color when you can use an entire rainbow?

Stress Alert: Discussions. Debates. Conflicts. Even the most calm, cool people need to blow off some steam every once in a while!

Tearjerker: Who doesn't like a good cry every now and then? In a *Trading Spaces* Reveal, sometimes they're tears of happiness, sometimes they're tears of sadness, but regardless of what emotion they display, they are the stuff legendary episodes are made of.

$\textcircled{?}$ **Good Idea?:** Sometimes projects don't quite work out as planned (drilling into rocks?), and sometimes questionable materials are used for a project (magazines as subflooring?). This icon denotes some of the most memorable.

Do you love how a room turned out? Dislike it? Somewhere in between? You have an opportunity to rate each and every room transformed on *Trading Spaces* with the super-easy Smiley-Face Rating Scale. Simply circle or fill in the face that corresponds with your opinion of each room.

Frank's Room:  | Laurie's Room: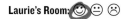

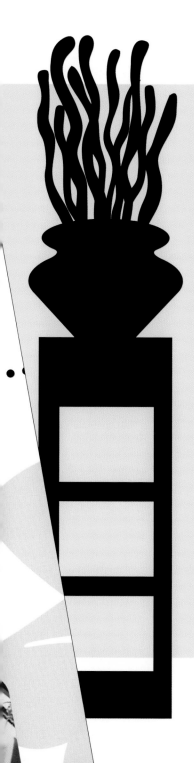

Season 1

Here's where it all began! In Season 1, we're introduced to Alex, Dez, Doug, Frank, Genevieve, Hildi, Laurie, Roderick, Vern, Amy Wynn, and Ty.

8 Designers

$80,000 Total Budget

First Designer Chat

First Budget Overrun

First Ceiling Fan Removed

40 Episodes

I Host

160 Homeowners

2 Carpenters

Series Debut

Voodoo Dolls

First Carpenter Consult

80 Room Transformations

8:11.05

01:05:11.02

04:48.21

:40:18.16

01:04:33.24

S1	
E1	

Knoxville, TN: Fourth & Gill

Cast: Alex, Frank, Laurie, Amy Wynn   Frank's Room: ☺ ☺ ☹ | Laurie's Room: ☺ ☺ ☹

after

The Rooms

In the premiere episode, Laurie punches up a bland kitchen by painting the walls electric pear, retiling the floor in large black and white checks, and using chrome accents. She also creates an organized family message and filing center. Frank brightens a den by using a faux-suede finish in shades of gold on the walls, reupholstering the homeowners' Arts and Crafts furniture, and painting two armoires in shades of red, gold, and black.

before

Welcome!

Kicking off the first episode in the series, Alex, Frank, Laurie, and Amy Wynn make their *Trading Spaces* debut.

DESIGNED BY LAURIE

Sticky Situation

Laurie runs into some time-management problems. Amy Wynn needs to saw the subflooring in the kitchen, but the walls have just been painted—and everyone's worried about getting sawdust stuck to the wet paint.

" **Wood Goddess.**
—What Frank calls Amy Wynn "

after

before

Tearjerker: The two female homeowners cry tears of happiness when they come together for the sign-off.

Super Sleuths

One set of homeowners gets some hints about what is happening in their house because Alex happens to mention work being done on their kitchen floor. Their suspicions are confirmed when the neighbors working on their home call them overnight because they don't have hot water. The homeowners deduce that the only way they would lose hot water in the kitchen would be from moving the refrigerator, which would have been done to work on the floor.

Huh?
Frank describes his paint choice as a "funky finish ... Macintosh era meets Howdy Doody."

Watch for:

Frank demonstrates the Frank Droop, meant to keep your arm from getting tired while painting. (It's a shoulder shimmy crossed with a slight back bend.)

S1
E2

Knoxville, TN: Forest Glen

Cast: Alex, Doug, Hildi, Amy Wynn

Doug's Room: ☺ 😐 ☹ | Hildi's Room: ☺ 😐 ☹

The Rooms

Doug creates a romantic bedroom, which he titles Country Urbane, by painting the walls sage green, building an upholstered bed, pickling (whitewashing) an existing vanity, and making a privacy screen. Hildi designs a sleek living room by painting the walls a dark putty color, sewing white slipcovers and curtains, hanging spotlights on the walls to showcase the homeowners' art, and building end tables that spin on lazy Susans.

Doug's Design Advice: "I think every room needs to have a sense of humor."

Welcome!
This episode is Doug and Hildi's *Trading Spaces* debut.

Notable
Doug has a couple of stressful moments: In one, he paces and repeatedly mumbles, "Why stress tomorrow when you can stress today?" In another, he walks off-camera and screams.

Crisis
Hildi creates controversy by wanting to paint a thin black stripe around the edge of the wood floor. Her homeowners are opposed to the idea and refuse to take any part in it. Regardless, she and Alex eventually do it.

Reveal-ing Moment
One of the living room homeowners starts to cry unhappy tears and exclaims, "Oh my God! They painted my floor!"

Athens, GA: County Road

S1 E3

💧 ✳ ⑦ | **Cast:** Alex, Frank, Hildi, Amy Wynn | Frank's Room: ☺ 😐 ☹ | Hildi's Room: ☺ 😐 ☹

after

01:39:28.20

DESIGNED BY HILDI

01:39:26.05

before

Trendsetter
Hildi becomes the first *Trading Spaces* designer to remove a ceiling fan.

The Rooms

Hildi updates a kitchen/living room area by painting the dark wood paneling and ceiling ecru, hanging cream draperies, slipcovering chairs with monkey-print fabric, building shelves to showcase the homeowners' pewter collection, and painting several pieces of furniture black. Frank brightens a child's room by painting the walls lavender, hanging a swing from the ceiling, making a wall-size art area with chalkboard spray paint, and spray-painting a mural of white trees.

Tearjerker: The female child's room homeowner cries tears of joy.

Safety First!

When Frank's female homeowner won't tie her hair back while spackling, he tells her that his hair is gone because of a bad spackling incident.

Is That Approved Usage?

Hildi enlarges the dining area of the room by ripping out a rounded portion of the carpet and laying vinyl tiles. To build up the tiles to the right height, she layers magazines as subflooring.

Hurry Up!
Frank falls behind on Day 2, so Alex takes the AlexCam around the neighborhood and gets shots of seniors saying that they've heard Frank might not finish on time.

01:43:05.12

after

DESIGNED BY FRANK

01:43:03.17

before

Age Matters

Frank is preoccupied with youth in this episode, noting that he's "a 5-year-old kid with chest hair." Later, while dealing with a nagging Alex: "Are you sure you aren't a reincarnated 2-year-old?" And, while describing the size of the swing seat to Amy Wynn: "Give me a 4-year-old heiny width."

S1 E4 | Alpharetta, GA: Providence Oaks

$? | **Cast:** Alex, Hildi, Roderick, Amy Wynn | **Hildi's Room:** ☺ ☺ ☹ | **Roderick's Room:** ☺ ☺ ☹

The Rooms

Roderick brightens a den/guest room by painting off-white stripes on the existing khaki walls, stenciling a sun motif in a deep rust-red, slipcovering the furniture with an off-white fabric, and installing a wall-length desk that can be hidden with curtains. Hildi re-creates a dining room using the existing dining table, aubergine paint, pistachio curtains, two-tone slipcovers, a striking star-shape light fixture, and a privacy screen.

Roderick

Aloha! This episode marks Roderick's only appearance on *Trading Spaces*.

Notable

Although he's never seen again on the show, Roderick is the first designer to use the term "homework" while talking to the homeowners about what needs to be done before the next morning. However, this is not the standard "homework assignment" scene that appears in later episodes.

Budget Buster

Roderick is $100 over budget.

Was It an Inch or a Foot?
Amy Wynn holds a pencil between her toes while measuring out the desk unit with Roderick.

Think It Will Hold?

Hildi attempts to create a heavy custom mirror by attaching mirrored squares on a flimsy luaun backing with liquid adhesive. She eventually gives up and pulls a mirror from another part of the house.

DESIGNED BY HILDI

Time Waster

Hildi, Alex, and Hildi's homeowners search for two days to find china—digging in the attic and asking the other homeowners where they store it—so they can set the table for The Reveal. They never find it.

Lawrenceville, GA: Pine Lane

S1 E5

$ ● ◇ | **Cast:** Alex, Dez, Hildi, Amy Wynn | Dez's Room: ☺ ☺ ☹ | Hildi's Room: ☺ ☺ ☹

DESIGNED BY HILDI

after

before

The Rooms

Hildi brings the outdoors in, creating an organically hip living room with a tree limb valance, wicker furniture, minty-white walls, and an armoire covered with dried leaves. Dez adds a feminine touch to a dark wood-paneled living room by whitewashing the walls, painting the fireplace, and dismantling a banister. She finds new ways to display the husband's taxidermy and decoy duck collection, which includes a custom duck lamp.

Fashion Report: Dez wears a porkpie hat during her Designer Chat.

Tag Team
One of Hildi's homeowners (who's working with her friend) becomes ill on Day 1, and her husband steps in to take her place.

Paint Problems
Dez's paint problems are complicated by one of her homeowners, who apparently spends both days priming and painting one built-in bookcase. His excuse: "Paint dries on its own time."

Wonder Woman
Amy Wynn demolishes Dez's banister, seemingly with her bare hands.

DEZ

Tearjerker: The homeowners who get Dez's room cry.

Budget Buster
Hildi winds up overbudget.

Back to the Drawing Board
Dez plans to install a mantel over the brick fireplace as the room's focal point, but the anchors she purchased won't work. The piece has to be scrapped, and she's disappointed.

after

before

Welcome!
This episode is Dez's *Trading Spaces* debut.

Buckhead, GA: Canter Road

S1
E6

Cast: Alex, Genevieve, Laurie, Amy Wynn | Genevieve's Room: ☺ ☺ ☹ | Laurie's Room: ☺ ☺ ☹

The Rooms

Gen gets wild in a kitchen by painting the walls electric pear, adding silver accents, using colanders as light covers, and removing cabinet doors. Laurie creates a crisp living room by painting the walls chocolate brown, laying a sea-grass rug, hanging a white frame on a large mirror, and adding cream and white slipcovers and curtains.

after

before

01:39:51.18

01:39:49.01

DESIGNED BY GENEVIEVE

Fashion Report: Gen is barefoot the entire episode.

01:04:48.21

Welcome!
This episode is Gen's *Trading Spaces* debut.

Things That Make You Go Hmmm...

Gen creates controversy when she decides to paint the existing Formica countertop with brown paint. Her homeowners aren't sure they like the results.

Bummer

Gen wants to change the flooring but doesn't have time. She expresses her disappointment by saying, "Linoleum bites."

01:39:46.05

after

Notable

The now famous Carpenter Consult scene debuts, with Laurie discussing her projects with Amy Wynn.

Demolition

Gen and Amy Wynn demolish a section of kitchen cabinets to make room for a pot hanger.

01:39:44.18

before

01:13:09.18

15

Washington, D.C.: Cleveland Park

Cast: Alex, Dez, Doug, Ty   Dez's Room: ☺ 😐 ☹ | Doug's Room: ☺ 😐 ☹

The Rooms

Doug goes retro in a basement by making a beanbag sofa and a kidney-shape coffee table and painting the walls bright orange. Dez creates a funky-festive living room by combining electric pear, white, gray, black, and red paint in solids, stripes, polka dots, and textured faux finishes.

The Name Game

This is the first *Trading Spaces* in which the host mentions the designers and carpenters while signing off.

Fashion Report: Doug wears dark angular glasses and has curly hair in this episode, and Dez sports a turban-inspired hat during her Designer Chat.

DESIGNED BY DOUG

after

before

>" I wish you spent as much time laying this project out as you did on your hair this morning. "
>
> —One of Doug's homeowners criticizing his "freeform planning"

Budget Crunch

Claiming he doesn't have enough money to buy legs for his coffee table, Doug substitutes plastic tumblers filled with plaster of Paris.

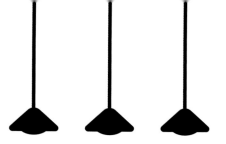

DEZ

`01:39:29.12.2`

before

`01:39:31.03.2`

▶ after

Mythical Masterpiece?
Dez creates a custom "Medusa lamp" featuring three heads, spiky lightbulbs, and Christmas lights.

Notable
One of Dez's young female homeowners is smitten with Ty and quickly volunteers to work with him on a project, leaving the remaining partner to say to Dez, "Who does she think she's kidding?"

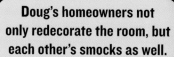

Doug's homeowners not only redecorate the room, but each other's smocks as well.

`01:25:51.04.2`

Welcome!
This episode is Ty's *Trading Spaces* debut.

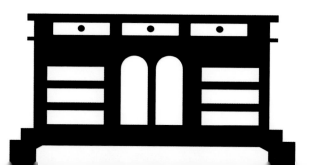

17

S1
E8

Alexandria, VA: Riefton Court

Cast: Alex, Frank, Genevieve, Ty   Frank's Room: ☺ ☺ ☹ | Genevieve's Room: ☺ ☺ ☹

DESIGNED BY FRANK

The Rooms

Frank cozies a country kitchen by creating a
picket-fence shelving unit and using seven pastel
paint colors to create a hand-painted quilt on
the walls. Gen goes graphic in a living room,
enlarging and recropping family photos, turning
an existing entertainment center on its side,
and painting the walls bright red.

after

before

Quotable Quotes
Frank's full of great lines in this episode.
Explaining his design: "I thought ... country
quilt. This looks like a quilt threw up in here,
but when you see the result, you're gonna
love it." Other notable quotes: "The only
thing we won't have in here is a cow,"
"Maybe we should just sort of cross our
legs and think about things," and "I'm
having a Tammy Faye moment."

> **Could it be because [at] the other house the individual is very tall, very gorgeous, and has enough sex appeal to knock over a troupe?**
> —Frank explains to Ty his theory on why Gen's projects are getting done and his are not

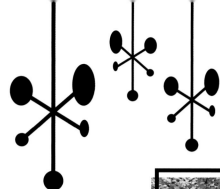

Coping with Anticipation

Gen's homeowners are excited and open the paint cans to see the color before Gen has a chance to reveal it.

Wood Woes

While drilling into the entertainment center, Gen talks about how soft the wood is—yet still manages to break her drill bit in it.

after

before

Gen's Design Advice

"I think it's always nice whenever you're going to change something in someone's house to leave something vaguely familiar so it's not going to be dramatic but there's something comforting as well."

DESIGNED BY GENEVIEVE

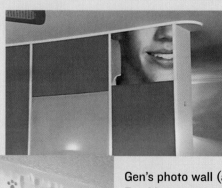

Gen's photo wall (above). Frank's country quilt paint treatment (left).

S1
E9

Annapolis, MD: Fox Hollow

Cast: Alex, Genevieve, Laurie, Ty

Genevieve's Room: ☺ 😐 ☹ | Laurie's Room: ☺ 😐 ☹

The Rooms

Laurie enlivens a drab kitchen with muted pumpkin paint, new light fixtures, and a custom pot hanger. Gen warms a living room with butterscotch paint, white curtains, framed family pictures, and a combination wood/carpet floor.

after

before

Limber Up!

Gen leads morning stretches with her homeowners before getting to work on Day 2.

She's Just Beginning ...
Laurie removes her first ceiling fan on the show.

Problem Solved!
Gen wants to hang the draperies using grommets. She and Alex have several giggle fits while trying various ways to attach them, but they can't seem to get them to work. Gen eventually figures it out on her own, and the draperies—complete with grommets—are featured during The Reveal.

after

before

Coincidence?
The paint colors that Gen and Laurie choose—butterscotch and muted pumpkin—are incredibly similar despite the different names.

Outta Here: Ty demolishes a railing in Gen's house.

Philadelphia, PA: Strathmore Road

S1
E10

$ | **Cast:** Alex, Dez, Frank, Amy Wynn | Dez's Room: ☺ ☺ ☹ | Frank's Room: ☺ ☺ ☹

after

DESIGNED BY FRANK

before

The Rooms

Frank goes earthy by painting a living room brown with a sueding technique. He also creates handmade accents, a child-size teepee, and a window seat with storage. Dez goes for "casual elegance" in a living room, using purple paint, a repeated gray harlequin diamond pattern on the walls, and an end table lamp made out of a trash can.

> ## "Beetlejuice lives here.
> —Homeowners' reaction to Dez's design"

DEZ

Quotable Quotes

Frank trying to figure out how comfortable a cushion is: "What's the heiny quotient on that?" Frank running out of time on Day 2: "I'm so tense ... you could literally use me as a paper press." Frank encouraging his male homeowner's craftier side: "It's just two guys [who,] instead of watching a football game and drinking chilled beverages, [are] painting boxes."

after

before

Trend Setter

Dez is the first *Trading Spaces* designer to be talked out of painting the fireplace by her homeowners.

Hue Hopping

Dez paints a wall bright purple, isn't sure about the hue, and goes back to the store to buy a darker version ("It was hideous."). Later on Day 2, she isn't happy with her light gray paint for the wall's harlequin pattern and wants to buy a darker shade, but Alex has to talk her out of it.

Budget Buster: Frank ends up 23 cents over budget.

21

S1
E11

Philadelphia, PA: Valley Road

Cast: Alex, Doug, Laurie, Amy Wynn   **Doug's Room:** ☺ ☺ ☹ | **Laurie's Room:** ☺ ☺ ☹

The Rooms

Doug softens a sunroom he names Blue Lagoon by painting the walls a deep robin's egg blue, painting blue and white diamonds on the hardwood floor, hanging whitewashed bamboo blinds, and adding pale yellow accents. He adds a *Rear Window* touch by placing a pair of binoculars (which he finds in the basement) in the sunroom so the homeowners can watch their children playing outside. Laurie goes Greek, painting a dining room deep russet with black and white accents, adding white Grecian urns, and even creating a white bust using one of her homeowners as a model.

DESIGNED BY DOUG

after

Tearjerker: The sunroom homeowners cry happy tears.

before

Four Out of Five Dentists Agree ...
Doug uses picture wire as dental floss. He doesn't recommend it.

The better to see you with ... (the binoculars from Doug's room).

`01:40:23.19`

after

`01:40:22.23`

before

`01:22:42.18`

Notable

Laurie thinks she's so ahead of schedule on Day 1 that she leads Doug to believe she's been asked to slow down and relax with the family dog so as not to finish too early. She then falls behind on Day 2 and becomes a bit anxious about finishing.

Greek God?

In order to make a Grecian bust to accessorize her room, Laurie convinces her male homeowner to take off his shirt, be wrapped in gooey papier mâché, and sit very still as it dries.

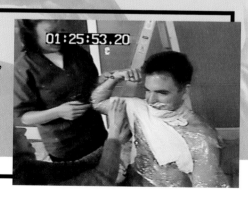

`01:25:53.20`

S1
E12

Philadelphia, PA: Galahad Road

($) | **Cast:** Alex, Genevieve, Hildi, Amy Wynn | Genevieve's Room: ☺ ☺ ☹ | Hildi's Room: ☺ ☺ ☹

The Rooms

Hildi warms a family-friendly living/dining room by introducing coffee-color walls, a midnight blue fireplace, a custom-built sectional couch, and zebra-stripe dining chair covers. Gen brightens a basement den by painting the walls lily pad green, adding orange accents, introducing a modern white couch, and weaving white fabric on the ceiling to cover the drop-ceiling tiles.

after

DESIGNED BY HILDI

Antici-paint-ion

Hildi's homeowners are too excited to wait for the paint reveal and open the cans themselves (much like Gen's homeowners in Alexandria: Riefton Court (Season 1, Episode 8).

before

Budget Buster
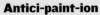

Hildi's design puts her over budget.

Notable

Hildi's homeowners are doubtful that their neighbors will like their new room; they challenge Hildi on most decisions.

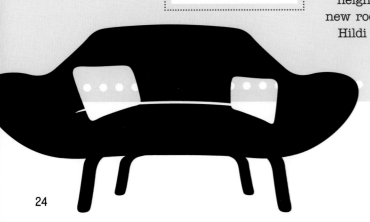

TCR 01:39.20:23

DESIGNED BY GENEVIEVE

after

TCR 01:39.17:22

before

Fashion Report: Gen wears a cowboy hat the entire episode.

TCR 01:12.22:15

WARNING
GIRL WITH ATTITUDE

Wily Wynn
Amy Wynn tells Alex that the coffee table she's constructing for Gen is "really, really ugly" and that she'd throw it out if it were in her room.

Wise Wynn
Gen plans to demolish an entire wall, but Amy Wynn talks her out of it due to structural concerns.

R 01:42.26:23

S1
E13

Knoxville, TN: Courtney Oak

$ ✳ | **Cast:** Alex, Frank, Laurie, Amy Wynn | Frank's Room: ☺ ☺ ☹ | Laurie's Room: ☺ ☺ ☹

The Rooms

Laurie goes organic by painting a bedroom a deep pistachio green, adding soft draperies, painting a vine around the vanity mirror, and using a cornice board to drape fabric on either side of the headboard. Frank gets in touch with his "inner child" by painting the walls of a basement light denim blue, freehanding murals of trees and flowers, and spray-painting fluffy white clouds.

01:38:51.18

after

DESIGNED BY LAURIE

Budget Buster

Laurie's design goes over budget.

01:38:49.12

before

01:38:56.04

after

Fan Debates

Laurie removes the ceiling fan. Alex argues with Frank about his decision to leave two brown ceiling fans in place. Frank defends his choice: "With people dying everywhere and starving children, really, two ceiling fans of the wrong color are minor trivialities."

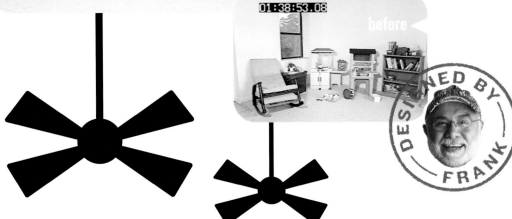

01:38:53.08

before

DESIGNED BY FRANK

S1
E14

Cincinnati, OH: Melrose Avenue

$ | **Cast:** Alex, Frank, Hildi, Ty | Frank's Room: ☺ ☺ ☹ | Hildi's Room: ☺ ☺ ☹

DESIGNED BY HILDI

after

before

The Rooms

Hildi gets crafty in a kitchen, creating her own wallpaper with tissue paper and flower stencils based on a fabric pattern. She installs a found dishwasher, extends the countertop, builds an island out of the kitchen table, paints the ceiling and the furniture yellow, and lays vinyl tile flooring. Frank adds soft, Victorian touches to a living room by exposing the existing wood floor, creating a faux-tin fireplace surround, painting a navy wall border with a rose motif, creating a fireplace screen that matches the border, and building a bench-style coffee table.

Pleasant Surprise

Frank rips out the existing carpet and finds a marble tile fireplace hearth that works well with his design.

Budget Buster

Frank's over budget.

DESIGNED BY FRANK

after

before

Love Connection?

Frank's male and female homeowners admit to crushes on Alex and Ty, respectively.

Notable

Frank admits to country-and-western dancing with his wife.

Cincinnati, OH: Sturbridge Road

S1
E15

Cast: Alex, Doug, Genevieve, Ty   Doug's Room: ☺ ☺ ☹   Genevieve's Room: ☺ ☺ ☹

The Rooms

Doug turns a dining room into a "Zen-Buddhist-Asian room" with a chocolate brown ceiling, warm honey-copper walls, Venetian plaster squares, and folded-metal-screen window treatments. Gen creates an Indian bedroom for a teenage girl by painting the walls with warm gold and red tones, hanging a beaded curtain, and creating a draped canopy.

after

01:40:09.16

01:40:07.03

before

Notable

Doug gives the first official homework assignment on the show.

Scary Stuff: Doug raps.

Fashion Report: Gen and her homeowners wear Indian forehead markings for inspiration.

Huh?

Gen describes her design theme as Trance-chill.

Quotable Quote

When Doug takes some of her lumber, Gen jokes dryly, "I think he's feeling insecure about his room or he's got a little crush on me and he's just really sad about the rejection."

Tearjerker

The bedroom homeowners cry tears of happiness upon seeing their newly decorated room.

01:40:13.15

after

01:40:12.01

before

Meeting of the Minds

Doug and Ty spend most of Day 1 discussing and redesigning Doug's plans for the dining room table. After several design tweaks from both, they agree to make it resemble a distressed picnic table.

It's in the Stars

Because the teenager is an Aries (a fire sign), Gen decides to use golds and yellows heavily throughout her design.

Cincinnati, OH: Madison & Forest

S1
E16

$ ○ ✳ | **Cast:** Alex, Doug, Laurie, Ty | **Doug's Room:** ☺ 😐 ☹ | **Laurie's Room:** ☺ 😐 ☹

Tearjerker: The bedroom homeowners cry happy tears.

after

before

It's so cold outside that Ty refers to his shop as an igloo.

The Rooms

Laurie warms a tiny bedroom with mustard yellow paint, a custom-built entertainment center, and a short suspended bed canopy. Doug transforms a Victorian living room into an industrial loft with multiple shades of purple paint, a yellow ceiling, custom art made from coordinating paint chips, wall sconces made of candy dishes, and a chair reupholstered in Holstein-print fabric.

It's Outta Here

Laurie nixes the existing ceiling fan.

Notable

This is the first episode in which both designers make a point of assigning homework and leaving for the evening.

DESIGNED BY LAURIE

DESIGNED BY DOUG

Yucky Moment

Doug rips out old carpet but isn't happy with the smell, calling it eau de cat.

Budget Buster

Doug goes $100 over budget.

after

before

HURRY UP!

Doug has his homeowners create art projects in a 10-minute time frame. Alex walks around with a stopwatch.

Tension

Doug and Ty don't see eye to eye while building a custom mirror that's too big to fit above the fireplace. Doug eventually takes full responsibility for the mirror dimensions.

San Diego, CA: Elm Ridge

S1
E17

⑦ ⑤ ♥ | **Cast:** Alex, Genevieve, Hildi, Amy Wynn | Genevieve's Room: ☺ ☺ ☹ | Hildi's Room: ☺ ☺ ☹

The Rooms

01:39:20.27 after

01:39:19.14 before

DESIGNED BY GENEVIEVE

In this infamous episode, Gen truly brings the outdoors in. She covers a bedroom wall with Oregon moss, lays a natural-tone tile floor, and adds a canopy that is lit from above with twinkling lights. Hildi works to convince her homeowners that they can brighten a bedroom by painting the walls and furniture midnight blue, adding zebra-stripe floor cubes, and using exposed subflooring in place of carpet.

Don't Rock the Boat
When the elder of Gen's father and son team (a naval officer) balks at covering the wall with moss, she tells him, "If you can protect our country, you can hang moss." He later complains that the moss "smells like somebody's old underwear."

Un-bear-able
One of Gen's male homeowners constantly carries around a teddy bear, setting the bear in various places throughout the room's transformation.

Tile Headaches
Due to time constraints, Gen chooses to lay floor tiles with liquid adhesive instead of tile adhesive and grout. Her team ends up re-laying many tiles during Day 2 because the adhesive doesn't quite work. Hildi's grout unexpectedly dries white—which clashes with the dark concrete tiles. Hildi improvises by knowingly going over budget to buy rugs. Bonus: Hildi drives off in a sporty silver convertible for her emergency shopping trip.

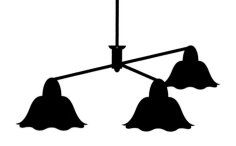

> **"** We have to give him the unexpected. It's very important in design. **"**
> —Hildi's design advice

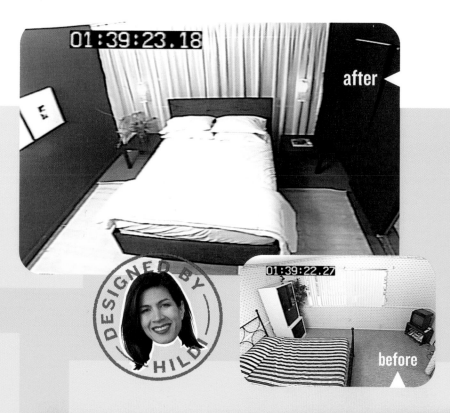

01:39:23.18

after

DESIGNED BY HILDI

01:39:22.27

before

If Only They'd Listened ...
Amy Wynn tells Alex that she tried to warn both designers that their plans for redoing the floors in both houses wouldn't go well. She then says that she doesn't like Hildi's floor and asks, "Is [Gen] trying to prove they can make a bedroom look like a patio?"

Shopping Savvy
Hildi shows viewers her bargaining strategy while shopping for lights.

Budget Buster: Hildi's last-minute rug purchase sends her budget over the $1,000 limit.

21

Busted
Hildi creates a copper mesh bust using herself as a model. The female homeowner isn't thrilled with the idea and says, "You went to design school?"

01:01:38.02

Notable

The ladies surf during B-Roll footage.

31

S1
E18

San Diego, CA: Hermes Avenue

$ | **Cast:** Alex, Genevieve, Laurie, Amy Wynn | Genevieve's Room: ☺ ☺ ☹ | Laurie's Room: ☺ ☺ ☹

The Rooms

Laurie brightens a kitchen by painting the walls Tiffany-box blue, installing a wooden slat grid system on one wall, hanging butter yellow draperies, building a banquette seating area, coating the stove in chrome-color paint, and painting the cabinets butter yellow. Gen uses Georgia O'Keeffe's Southwestern paintings as inspiration for transforming a living room. She paints the walls clay red, hangs a cow skull above the fireplace, adds a woven rug, hangs new light fixtures, frames large black-and-white cropped photos of the homeowners' children, builds a distressed coffee table with firewood legs, and covers the existing baby bumpers with crafts fur.

Reveal-ing Moment: The female living room homeowner is so excited about her room that she picks up Alex—twice.

Resourceful

Laurie reframes a wide off-center window by covering it with a larger centered wood frame and nailing bamboo place mats to the frame to cover the window blinds.

Watch Your Step
Gen accidentally steps into a bucket of spackling compound and must hop around on one foot until one of her homeowners brings her a towel.

Carpentry Conflict

Laurie wants all of her carpentry projects completed by the end of Day 1. Amy Wynn makes an executive decision and tells her no.

Budget Buster
Laurie can't afford to spend money on cabinet hardware, so her homeowners ask for permission to buy it themselves as a gift for their friends. Laurie agrees. During Designer Chat, Alex says that she'll bend the rules once for Laurie, but never again.

S1 E19

San Diego, CA: Wilbur Street

$ | **Cast:** Alex, Doug, Frank, Amy Wynn | **Doug's Room:** ☺ 😐 ☹ | **Frank's Room:** ☺ 😐 ☹

after

before

DESIGNED BY FRANK

The Rooms

Frank mixes British Colonial and tropical looks in a living room with soft mauve paint, exposed wood flooring, several flowerpots and vases, and a custom architectural piece. Doug updates a dark kitchen with a Tuscan Today theme, using Venetian plaster tinted Tuscan Mango (OK, it's orange), painting the cabinets white and orange, and installing wood flooring.

before

DESIGNED BY DOUG

Yucky Moment

Alex helps Frank hot-glue moss to flowerpots and manages to lay her entire palm on a freshly glued spot. She gets glue and moss stuck to her hand, and Frank runs off to find first aid.

Quotable Quotes

Frank-isms abound in this episode. Frank on his wall hanging: "OK, now we're gonna make a metal taco." Frank on how tired he feels: "If someone invited me out to dinner, I'd have to hire someone to chew my food." And Frank on his finished room: "You could get malaria in this room it's so tropical."

after

Flooring Follies

Doug originally wants to install a parquet floor with 4x4-inch squares. Amy Wynn cuts 250 squares, but they cover only one-eighth of the floor. Amy has to stop cutting because the saw burns out. Doug winds up purchasing prefab flooring.

Budget Buster: Doug spends more than the allotted $1,000 on his design.

Making an Episode

● ●

It takes a village to raise a child ...

and likewise it takes the cast, homeowners, producers, sound and camera technicians, makeup assistants, and many more dedicated individuals to ensure each and every episode of *Trading Spaces* comes together. From start to finish, here's how it's done.

Start

Sign Up: Interested homeowners sign up online at www.tlc.com. Rooms should be at least 14' x 12'. The homeowners must be willing to sign away any right to sue for things they don't like.

Screening: Potential homeowners are thoroughly screened. The best way to be selected is to act like your goofy self. For example, one couple wore T-shirts featuring large silk-screen noses and the phrase "Pick us."

Match-up: Designers are matched up with rooms (and no, you can't pick your designer). With only a handful of photos of the selected room and a 20-minute video of the homeowners, the designers have two to three weeks to figure out their design plans and how to achieve them in a distant location.

Paint Reveal: The spontaneous slapping of paint onto walls is actually a carefully calculated shot. By noon, most rooms already have a first coat of paint, and the main carpentry or sewing projects have begun.

Load Out: The designer and homeowners miraculously clear an entire room in 30 seconds or less. (Production assistants carry off items and put them into temporary storage in a spare bedroom or garage. Amazingly, the entire process takes only about 15 minutes.)

Meet-and-Greet: The homeowners describe what they'd like to see happen in their neighbors' room, and then the designers tell the homeowners what they're planning to do. If there's going to be tension between the designers and homeowners, it'll start popping up about now.

Day 2

Special Segments: Sewing, painting, building, or arts and crafts projects can take 45 minutes to an hour to film. Why? Often a project is filmed several times. Attention may be focused on different aspects of the project, verbal instructions, or details regarding hands, tools, and materials.

Homework: On-camera it may appear as if the designer is leaving for the night; in reality, most of the cast and crew stay to help the homeowners complete the assigned tasks.

More Work: Designers meet with their homeowners to discuss what did (and didn't) get done the previous evening. Time and work usually begin to wear on the homeowners at this point. Paige assesses the homeowners' mental and physical condition.

overhead cam

Day 0

Arrival: The *Trading Spaces* crew rolls into town. You may be watching for a caravan of decorating superstars; what you'll see instead is a travel trailer hooked up to a 4 x 4 truck. The whole ensemble is about the size of a trailer you'd choose to move from your first apartment.

Filming Begins: The cast and crew film all the events that make up the start of a show (called B-Roll), from Paige's first lines to those goofy segments in which the cast horses around at some geographically significant site.

Home Visit: The cast and crew visit the homes. Both designers sit down with the carpenter for the show and hash out what's going to happen during the next two days.

Day 1

Show Time: Bright and early the homeowners join Paige outside and perform the sacred Key Swap. During breaks Paige gives the homeowners a pep talk on how to look natural on-camera and how to make the show fun. They often have to do the swap multiple times for technical reasons (i.e., a helicopter flies overhead).

Shopping Time: The designers and carpenters brave rabid fans, traffic jams, dwindling funds, and a strange, new town in their quest for the wood, paint, hardware, fabric, furniture, and accessories they'll need to transform their spaces.

Load In: This is the opposite of Load Out. Paige films a few "Hurry Up" scenes, in which she pushes designers and homeowners to speedily put on the finishing touches.

Designer Chat: Paige interviews each designer. During this segment, Paige and the designer highlight the key projects, as well as discuss the trials and tribulations associated with transforming the room.

The Reveal: The climax of three days of hard work. Because the homeowners' reactions can't be filmed a second time, lighting, sound, and camera angles must be perfect. Often, cast and crew watch the reactions on a video monitor.

Finish

Knoxville, TN: Stubbs Bluff

$ | **Cast:** Alex, Doug, Frank, Ty | **Doug's Room:** ☺ ☺ ☹ | **Frank's Room:** ☺ ☺ ☹

The Rooms

Frank lets the ideas flow while punching up a basement with a karaoke stage, a tiki hut bar, and several other tropical accents—including a canoe for seating. Doug brings a farmhouse kitchen up-to-date by painting the walls a muted coffee color, adding sage and lilac accents, building benches in the dining area, hanging silver cooking utensils on the painted cabinet fronts, and laying vinyl tile.

01:40:18.16

after

before

01:40:17.10

DESIGNED BY FRANK

Daily Source of Fiber?

Frank gnaws off a tree branch with his teeth.

01:39:04.29

Budget Buster: Frank goes over budget creating the tiki extravaganza.

01:05:11.02

Quotable Quotes

Frank comments on Ty's mellow attitude, saying, "He goes through like life's little pixie, like a little gnome looking for a mushroom." While explaining a crafts project to Alex, Frank suggests she make hers look like "you just went to the jungle and knocked over a monkey and dug up the soil and put it on a pot."

Fashion Report

Frank wears a hula outfit—complete with coconut bra—and asks, "Am I showing too much cleavage? Be honest."

Dutiful Doug

During the hurry-up shots at the end of the episode, Doug thoughtfully remembers to put out food for the homeowners' cat.

after

before

DESIGNED BY DOUG

The Name Game

Doug titles his room Cocteau Country based on the artist Jean Cocteau. He had hoped his plaster-coated pitchfork and shovel would be reminiscent of Cocteau's work.

Plaster Problems

Even though Doug and Alex spend much of the episode mixing plaster to coat a shovel and a pitchfork to hang on the wall, the plaster won't dry fast enough, so Doug eventually spray-paints the tools instead.

" You're gonna have to change from total professional to sleaze ball. "

—Frank trying to put Ty in the right frame of mind to envision his design

Miami, FL: 168th/83rd Streets

→ ◊ ? | **Cast:** Alex, Dez, Laurie, Ty   Dez's Room: ☺ ☺ ☹ | Laurie's Room: ☺ ☺ ☹

after

before

The
Rooms

Dez adds drama to a bedroom by applying a "pan-Asian ethnic theme," featuring upholstered cornice boards, mosquito netting, and stenciled dragon lampshades. Laurie warms up a living room by painting the walls brick red with black and cream accents, building two large bookcases, hanging botanical prints, slipcovering the existing furniture, and using a faux-tortoiseshell finish on a coffee table.

DEZ

Oink?

Dez adds a large pink piggy bank that she dressed in a skirt and a wig.

Notable

Dez falls ill with the flu on Day 2 and spends a lot of time sleeping on a couch. As a result, her team falls behind. Ty jumps in to help finish the room on time.

Fashion Report: Ty wears flip-flops in the shop.

So Stylish!

Dez wears an amazing large-brimmed hat during Designer Chat. It features black and white spots, fuzzy black trim, and a very tall white feather. She's outdone herself.

38

after

before

01:43:18.09

01:43:16.18

Fireplace Fiasco

Laurie's homeowners want to install a faux fireplace, and she vetoes it. The homeowners convince Ty to help them build a square frame and paint logs and a fire on it. They keep putting it in the room, and Laurie keeps removing it.

A Puzzling Way to Spend Time

Because Laurie knows her homeowners love puzzles, she buys several to accessorize the room. Most stay in boxes, but she expects her team to put a large 3-D puzzle together for The Reveal—in addition to their other work. There are several shots of everyone working on it at different times, but it never comes together.

Tearjerker: The living room homeowners cry.

01:04:28.28

Laurie creates a faux-tortoiseshell effect on a coffee table.

01:29:47.28

Musical Moments

Laurie plays "Chopsticks" on the homeowners' piano.

S1
E22

Fort Lauderdale, FL: 59th Street

(\$) ✳ | **Cast:** Alex, Frank, Hildi, Ty   Frank's Room: ☺ 😐 ☹ | Hildi's Room: ☺ 😐 ☹

The Rooms

Hildi goes retro in a Fiestaware collector's kitchen by building an acrylic table, adding period chairs, and hanging large globe light fixtures. She also installs a shelving unit to display the homeowner's collection. Frank adds "comfortable drama" to a living room, with bright orange textured walls, a mosaic-top coffee table, slipcovered furniture, and a large custom art project.

01:39:24.15

after

DESIGNED BY HILDI

01:39:22.20

before

01:37:59.13

Budget Buster

Hildi's Fiestaware kitchen sets her back more than $1,000.

Girl Power: Hildi and her female homeowner use a blowtorch to smooth the edges on the acrylic dining table.

Going, Going, Gone

Hildi takes down the existing ceiling fan and hangs a large white globe light fixture in its place.

No table dances until February.

—Hildi to her homeowners
after completing the
acrylic table project

after

before

DESIGNED BY FRANK

Resourceful

Frank creates a large custom art piece using three wooden doors because they're cheaper than buying similar-size canvases.

Rest Assured

When Alex wants to break the tiles for Frank's coffee table project, she tells Ty and Frank that they don't let her do many heavy-duty tasks because they think of her as a lady. Frank reassures her, "You being a lady has never crossed my mind."

Quotable Quote

Frank describes his coffee table design to Ty by saying, "If you were in Pompeii just before Vesuvius erupted and you grabbed a piece of furniture, it would be this table."

Design Insight

During Designer Chat, Alex points out that one of the legs on Frank's coffee table is a slightly different style than the other three. Frank claims that he designs all his furniture that way.

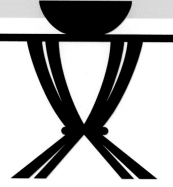

41

Key West, FL: Elizabeth Street

$ | **Cast:** Alex, Frank, Genevieve, Ty   Frank's Room: ☺ ☺ ☹ | Genevieve's Room: ☺ ☺ ☹

The Rooms

Gen makes a tiny living room appear larger with her Caribbean Chill design, which includes magenta walls with lime green accents, a large custom-built sectional sofa, and a wall decoupaged with pages torn from a 100-year-old book. Frank adds a Caribbean touch to a living room by painting the walls light blue, adding a hand-painted mermaid, building a telephone table, and laying vinyl tiles.

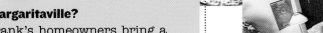

Last-Minute Trips

Both Gen and Frank do some emergency shopping on Day 2. Because she didn't have enough pages from an antique book to cover an entire wall, Gen runs out to buy a modern paperback and tea-dyes the pages to match. Frank sends one of his homeowners off on his bike to the local hardware store to buy hinges.

Budget Buster?

Gen's budget isn't discussed during the Designer Chat, but there's the unspoken idea that she may be over the spending limit.

Margaritaville?

Frank's homeowners bring a blender with them, because they never travel without it. The morning of Day 2 they admit to not finishing their homework, claiming a neighbor came over with champagne.

Thanks for the Tip!

Frank tells Alex to use a hair dryer to get rid of the hot glue "spider webs" on a project (by blowing the hair dryer on the area until they're gone).

S1
E24

Austin, TX: Wycliff

Cast: Alex, Doug, Hildi, Amy Wynn   Doug's Room: ☺ ☺ ☹ | Hildi's Room: ☺ ☺ ☹

after

before

DESIGNED BY HILDI

The Rooms

Hildi adds drama to a dining room by covering the walls with brown felt, papering the ceiling with small, individual red and gold squares, covering the back of an armoire with dried bamboo leaves, and making custom light fixtures. Doug creates a funky kitchen by painting the cabinets with blue and purple swirls, extending the existing countertop, applying blue and purple vinyl squares on the wall, and hanging numerous clocks (he titles the room Time Flies).

Fashion Report: Alex wears a leopard-print cowboy hat.

Time Flies

Doug covers a wall with clocks set for different time zones around the world. When one homeowner asks where the clock batteries are, Doug realizes that he forgot to buy them and that he doesn't have money left to get any. He decides to set and hang the clocks, even though they aren't running.

Job Description?

At the start of the show, Doug hasn't created any drawings or taken any measurements and expects Amy Wynn to cut all new cabinet doors by removing the old doors and tracing around them as templates. Amy Wynn complains to Alex that Doug thinks a carpenter is merely an assistant to a designer. Later Amy Wynn makes a point of thanking Hildi for her detailed drawings.

after

before

DESIGNED BY DOUG

Budget Buster
Doug spends more than the $1,000 limit.

Notable: Viewers see Hildi and Doug shopping together at the start of the episode.

S1	
E25	

Austin, TX: Wing Road

$ 💣✴   ✻ | **Cast:** Alex, Genevieve, Hildi, Amy Wynn   **Genevieve's Room:** ☺ 😐 ☹ | **Hildi's Room:** ☺ 😐 ☹

The
Rooms

Gen goes south of the border in a kitchen by adding a mosaic tile backsplash, covering the cabinet door insets with textured tin, painting the floors a terra-cotta color, and painting the walls yellow. Hildi brightens a living room by applying a textured glaze over the existing gold paint, covering a wall in wooden squares, sewing silver slipcovers, and adding a cowhide rug.

Change of Heart

Gen overcomes her distaste of linoleum (remember Buckhead: Canter Road (Season 1, Episode 6?) by stripping, painting, and sealing the existing linoleum floor. She's very pleased with the result.

01:39:52.08   after

01:39:48.19

before

DESIGNED BY GENEVIEVE

01:22:15.25

Love Notes

Gen's male homeowner has a crush on Amy Wynn. Gen and the homeowner's wife tease him repeatedly in front of Amy Wynn.

Fan Ban: Gen removes her first ceiling fan. Hildi removes her ceiling fan too.

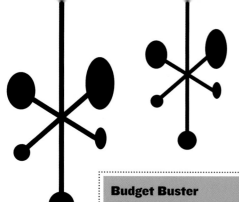

after

Budget Buster
Hildi goes over budget creating her lush room.

01:44:01.07

DESIGNED BY HILDI

01:43:59.22

before

01:33:17.00

Demolition

Gen and Amy Wynn destroy the inside shelves of a cabinet to create a small bar.

Seven Years' Bad Luck?
Gen planned on having a large mirror on the wall framed by patterned tin, but she claimed the mirror broke while driving around with Hildi. She hangs the frame anyway.

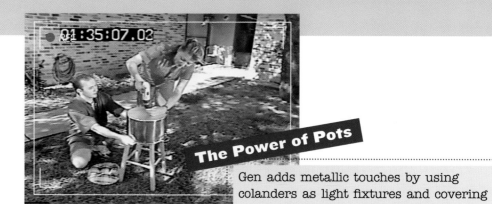

01:35:07.02

The Power of Pots

Gen adds metallic touches by using colanders as light fixtures and covering a bar stool with a tall pasta pot.

Fashion Report: Amy Wynn wears two braids in her hair.

S1	
E26	

Austin, TX: Birdhouse Drive

Cast: Alex, Frank, Laurie, Amy Wynn   Frank's Room: ☺ ☺ ☹ | Laurie's Room: ☺ ☺ ☹

The Rooms

Frank enlivens a living room by painting three walls sage green and the fireplace wall shocking pink, installing floor-to-ceiling shelving on either side of the fireplace, adding a hand-painted checkerboard table, and making unique art pieces. Laurie divides a living/dining room with a suspended piece of fabric, paints the rooms with warm oranges and yellows, adds olive green accents, builds a bench seat, and creates a custom coffee table.

01:39:42.04   after

01:39:40.04   before

Notable: Amy Wynn plays the saw.

Huh?
Frank describes a wooden rooster he wants to make as "kind of a Frenchy, Mediterranean slash funk Texas rooster."

01:39:45.29   after

Still Learning ...

Laurie learns the hard way that a large part of faux finishing is trial and error. She eventually says she'll have to talk to Frank about how to get the right effect.

01:39:45.03   before

Time Crunch
During Designer Chat, Laurie confesses that she was running short on time and that the paint on the bench she and Alex are sitting on is still tacky. Laurie gets a little nervous because she thinks she's sticking.

Yum: Laurie's homeowners entice Laurie to take a break to enjoy Mexican food from a local restaurant.

Orlando, FL: Lake Catherine

S1
E27

Cast: Alex, Hildi, Vern, Ty

Hildi's Room: ☺ ☺ ☹ | Vern's Room: ☺ ☺ ☹

01:39:43.00 after

DESIGNED BY VERN

01:39:40.28 before

Welcome: This episode is Vern's *Trading Spaces* debut.

The Rooms

Vern brings warmth and depth into a wine importer's kitchen by painting the walls with two shades of red, installing a custom-built wine rack, building a new chandelier using 36 wineglasses, and creating a new tabletop. Hildi creates a sleek bedroom with gray walls, an aluminum foil ceiling, gray flannel curtains, bamboo curtain rods, and a black armoire covered in bamboo.

● ●

> " [I want to give people] cleaner spaces and cleaner lines. "
>
> —Vern

Them's the Breaks

Vern can't seem to get a break—or maybe he gets too many. Many sconces he ordered were delivered broken and had to be epoxied. At the end of Day 2, one of Vern's homeowners juggles lemons and then breaks the vase he's putting them into.

Notable

Viewers are quickly introduced to Vern's perfectionist side:
1) He gives Ty several architectural drawings for what he wants created in the room. 2) After applying five coats of paint, he and his homeowners are still painting late on Day 2.

Do-over!

Alex causes paint problems for Vern by messing up the paint job on one of the kitchen stools. He makes her repaint it.

01:40:30.18 after

Tweet Dreams

Hildi includes a live canary in her design and names the bird Hildi.

DESIGNED BY HILDI

01:40:28.29 before

S1 E28 Orlando, FL: Gotha Furlong

 Cast: Alex, Frank, Genevieve, Ty   Frank's Room: ☺ ☺ ☹   Genevieve's Room: ☺ ☺ ☹

The Rooms

Gen creates romance in a bedroom by adding a ceiling-height cedar plank headboard, butter yellow paint, throw pillows made from a 1970s tablecloth, and cedar bookshelves. Frank makes a bedroom feel "earthy, arty, and wonderful" by painting the walls tan, adding gauzy white fabric to the four-poster bed, building a cedar window seat with storage drawers, painting a floorcloth, and hand-painting batik-print pillows.

after

before

DESIGNED BY

Problem Solved!

Gen tries to modify a ceiling fan by removing the existing blades and replacing them with woven fans. That doesn't work, so she uses silver rub on the blades (which adds a silver sheen to the wood grain) and rehangs them.

Notable

Gen's yellow paint gets on Alex's white pants. Alex then covers up the spot with gaffer's tape and explains to viewers that she did it so the other homeowners won't know what's happening in their home when she goes to help Frank.

Coincidence: Gen and one of her homeowners attended the same art school but at different times.

before

01:41:01.11

after

DESIGNED BY FRANK

Just Can't Get Enough

Alex catches Frank's homeowners watching an episode of *Trading Spaces* on TV while taking a break.

Frank paints Alex's nails and says that he does the same for his wife all the time.

01:29:40.13

TX E100S

01:13:34.22

19

19A

19

Frank demonstrates the batiking technique to his homeowners.

Reveal-ing Moment

When Alex reveals Frank's new bedroom to the homeowners, they like the design, but the husband worries that it's "a woman's room."

49

S1
E29

Orlando, FL: Winterhaven

Cast: Alex, Doug, Laurie, Ty

Doug's Room: ☺ ☺ ☹ | Laurie's Room: ☺ ☺ ☹

The Rooms

Laurie perks up a seldom-used living room with yellow paint, sheer window treatments, a geometric wall design, and a large ottoman. Doug regresses to his childhood while decorating a boy's bedroom. Doug's design, Americana Medley, includes red walls, a blue ceiling, stenciled stars and cow prints, a tree limb headboard, and a barn door window treatment.

TCR 01:40.31:05
after

TCR 01:40.30:02
before

DESIGNED BY LAURIE

TCR 01:13.59:2?

Up You Go!
One of Laurie's homeowners is afraid of heights, yet Laurie keeps putting him on ladders.

You Don't Say?
Doug gives the longest definition of a stencil known to man. It's too long to even recount here.

R 01:43.48:2?

One Satisfied Customer

The preteen who resides in the bedroom is very pleased. Upon seeing it his mouth falls open, his eyes get wide, and he can't seem to speak.

50

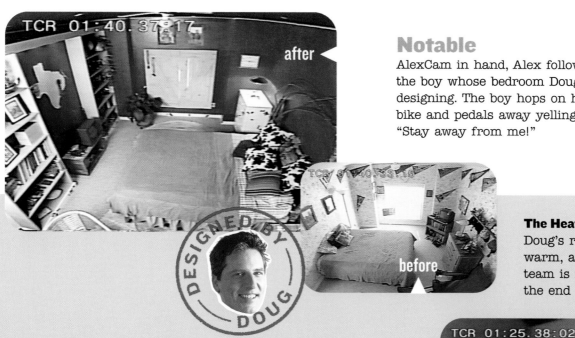

after

before

DESIGNED BY DOUG

Notable

AlexCam in hand, Alex follows the boy whose bedroom Doug is designing. The boy hops on his bike and pedals away yelling, "Stay away from me!"

The Heat Is On

Doug's room becomes very warm, and everyone on the team is incredibly sweaty by the end of Day 2.

The Name Game: Ty tells Alex that Doug's full name is Douglas Issues Wilson.

Poor Baby

Doug lies on the couch and pretends to pout because he didn't have his own bedroom growing up.

Sing Out

One of Doug's homeowners turns 40. The cast brings him a cake and sings "Happy Birthday." Doug takes the harmony.

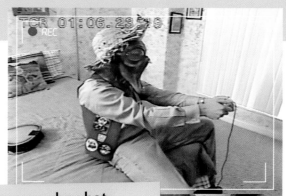

Fashion Report: Doug wears a red scouting vest during Day 1; Ty dons a cowboy hat.

The Key Swap

This is the point where the host crosses her arms and gives each set of homeowners the keys to each other's home so they can trade spaces for the duration of filming. Sometimes the homeowners hold personal items (espresso maker, anyone?), sometimes they don't; sometimes the group stands in front of the homes, sometimes it doesn't (grab a paddle for a quick ride in a canoe!). Regardless of what the homeowners do—or don't do—this is the official kickoff of each and every episode. Here are some favorite Key Swaps.

Lizard Love

One homeowner holds a large lizard and hands it to Paige as he leaves to go to the other home. (California: Via Jardin, Season 3, Episode 51)

Isn't That Cute?

One homeowner carries a teddy bear, which Alex holds and returns to the homeowner after the swap. (San Diego, CA: Elm Ridge, Season I, Episode 17)

Tanks a Lot ...

Paige wears a tank top that reads Key Swap. (New York: Whitlock Road, Season 3, Episode 6)

Hmmm ...

One homeowner carries a blender, and the homeowners on the other team are on bicycles. (Key West, FL: Elizabeth Street, Season I, Episode 23)

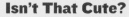

Paddle Swap?

The homeowners swap keys while sitting in canoes as Paige stands on a dock. After switching keys, the homeowners paddle to each other's home. (Miami, FL: Ten Court, Season 3, Episode 43)

One Shot or Two?

One homeowner carries an espresso maker.
(Seattle, WA: 56th Place, Season 2, Episode 23)

Balcony Buzz

After the Key Swap, Paige stands on a balcony between the homeowners' residences (they live on two different levels of a complex). Paige is nearly attacked by bees after the homeowners head to each other's residence. (Providence, RI: Phillips Street, Season 2, Episode 5)

That's a First!

In this episode, Paige doesn't hold the keys. Instead, she holds a dry-erase board on which she has drawn football plays, and the homeowners switch keys with each other. (Virginia: Gentle Heights Court, Season 3, Episode 17)

This Episode's Gone to the Birds!

One homeowner carries a large bird cage containing two birds. (Scottsdale, AZ: Bell Road, Season 3, Episode 38)

Light My Way!

The female homeowners present Paige with a small lamp.
(Plano, TX: Shady Valley Road, Season 2, Episode 41)

S1

E30

Albuquerque, NM: Gloria

Cast: Alex, Doug, Hildi, Ty | **Doug's Room:** ☺ ☺ ☹ | **Hildi's Room:** ☺ ☺ ☹

The Rooms

Doug sets sail in a living room (Wind in Our Sails) by painting the walls slate gray, hanging white curtains, installing a banquette, and suspending a large white canvas from the ceiling. Hildi warms up a living room by painting the walls copper and red, painting the sofas brown, making a curtain rod from copper pipe, and creating cubes that are hung on the wall as an entertainment center.

Notable: Hildi, Doug, and Ty frolic on playground equipment during B-Roll shots.

Fashion Report

The female homeowners sport blue and green nail polish and nail art that spells out *Trading Spaces*.

Notable 2

Alex sings (off-key) and plays guitar for Doug. Doug responds by singing her a song: "Alex is gonna go places we don't want to go. She's gonna be lonely there, singing her sad, sad songs."

Lucky Break

Hildi's homeowners convince her to rip up the existing carpet. She is pleasantly surprised by the brown tile underneath, which goes perfectly with her design.

Santa Fe, NM: Felize

S1
E31

Cast: Alex, Genevieve, Vern, Ty

Genevieve's Room: ☺ ☺ ☹ | Vern's Room: ☺ ☺ ☹

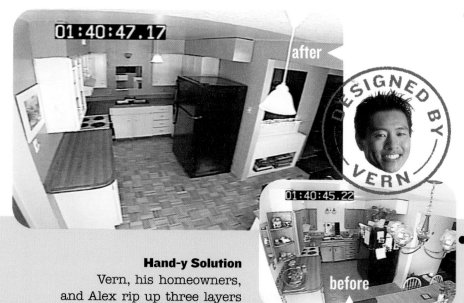

The Rooms

Vern creates a calming oasis in a kitchen by painting the walls pale blue, installing a planter of wheatgrass, laying parquet flooring, hanging mirrors, and applying a stained-glass-looking treatment to the cabinet doors. Gen designs a modern Southwestern living room (Adobe Mod) by adding white paint, a custom-built sofa, woven-rope end tables, and clay jars.

Hand-y Solution

Vern, his homeowners, and Alex rip up three layers of linoleum flooring to lay the parquet flooring. Alex speeds up the process by prying up large portions of the floor with a hand truck.

Good for You?

Vern tastes the wheatgrass, hates it, and tries to spit it out. Alex makes a wheatgrass smoothie and hates it too.

Notable

Gen, Vern, and Ty ride horses during their introduction.

Under the Wire

Having just completed Gen's coffee table, Ty brings it into the room after both sets of homeowners have come back together. He's in the shot for the sign-off.

A Nod to Tradition

Gen's homeowners smudge the room with sage, a Native American practice, after clearing the furniture from the room.

S1
E32

New Orleans, LA: Jacob Street

| 💣 💧 💲 | **Cast:** Alex, Hildi, Laurie, Amy Wynn | Hildi's Room: ☺ 😐 ☹ | Laurie's Room: ☺ 😐 ☹ |

The Rooms

Hildi modernizes a kitchen by painting the walls pistachio green, laying black vinyl tile, building a new island, and using plumbing conduit as shelving supports. Laurie creates continuity and flow in a kitchen/office/dining/living room, using pale yellow paint on the walls, a 20-foot-long sisal rug, slipcovers, new kitchen storage, and a new furniture arrangement.

after

before

DESIGNED BY HILDI

Demolition

Hildi and her homeowners do some heavy demolition by knocking out a large existing island and several kitchen cabinets.

Running on Empty

Hildi's homeowners were literally up all night doing homework and are working without any sleep on Day 2.

after

before

Witchy-Poo

In the spirit of New Orleans, Alex cuts locks of hair from Hildi and Laurie to make voodoo dolls. Hildi is nonchalant about the hair loss, but Laurie isn't pleased. After making the dolls, Alex sticks each doll in the rear end to make the designers hurry up.

Notable

The owners of the multipurpose living room—both the husband and the wife—cry tears of happiness. For Laurie, this is the most memorable *Trading Spaces* Reveal, because "the family was deeply moved and appreciated what we did."

Spreading It Thin: Laurie runs out of paint and can't buy more because she's completely out of money.

New Orleans, LA: Walter Road

S1
E33

Cast: Alex, Frank, Genevieve, Amy Wynn

Frank's Room: ☺ ☹ ☹ | Genevieve's Room: ☺ ☹ ☹

The Rooms

Frank updates a kitchen by removing garish wallpaper, coating the walls with textured tan paint, painting the cabinet drawers red and green, coiling copper wire around the existing drawer pulls, and installing a large bulletin board to help keep the family organized. Gen creates an antique look in a bedroom she titles Bombay Meets Étouffée. She paints the walls peach and pea green, installs a vintage beaded chandelier, and applies an antiqued gold finish to cornice boards and bookshelves.

Measuring Up
Frank measures a space in a room by lying on the floor and stretching his arms over his head. He tells Amy Wynn the length is "one fat man with arms extended."

Quotable Quotes
It's a tie between Frank and, well, Frank. On the challenge of finishing on budget: "I feel like someone's given me a wad of chewing gum and said, 'Go fill up the Grand Canyon'."; on the public's perception of designers: "If somebody tells me that a designer is just this little guy who goes around fluffing flowers, I intend to break every bone in his body and make a lamp out of him."

Fashion Report
Gen reveals her numerous fabrics to the homeowners by walking into the room wearing the different cloths around her head, waist, and arms.

New Orleans, LA: D'evereaux Street

? | **Cast:** Alex, Genevieve, Vern, Amy Wynn | Genevieve's Room: ☺ ☺ ☹ | Vern's Room: ☺ ☺ ☹

The Rooms

Gen heads back to the 1960s in her Retro Fly den/guest room by painting multicolor stripes on the walls, hanging retro light fixtures, slipcovering an existing futon, and separating the desk area from the seating area with a chain-link screen. Vern kicks up the style in a bedroom shared by two young brothers with a black and white soccer theme. He paints the walls black and white, upholsters the headboards, creates two desk stations, suspends soccer balls from the ceiling, and lays a black and white vinyl floor complete with a custom soccer ball medallion.

Grab Some Caulk ...

Gen and her homeowners have problems finding wall studs. When their electronic stud finder stops working, they start drilling random holes to find the studs.

Quotable Quote

Vern consults with the younger boy, Scotty, at the start of the show. Scotty tells Vern he wants to become an architect. Vern gives him a high five and tells him that "[Architects] get all the women."

Male Bonding?

Vern and his male homeowner fondly reminisce about having *the* Farah poster in each of their rooms while growing up.

Just Kidding!

Alex plays soccer with the two little boys and tells them that the girls in their classes at school will love the new bedroom because it's a "girlie room." The boys knock her to the ground.

S1
E35

New York: Shore Road

♦ ♥ | **Cast:** Alex, Dez, Genevieve, Amy Wynn | Dez's Room: ☺ ☺ ☹ | Genevieve's Room: ☺ ☺ ☹

after

01:40:46.1

01:40:44.29

before

The
Rooms

Gen looks to the East for inspiration on a sunporch and creates a tearoom atmosphere with a new sake bar, a seating area, and several organic accents. Dez gives a living room her version of "country with a French twist" by painting the walls yellow, stenciling fern leaves around the room, slipcovering the existing sofa, adding a planter of grass, and hanging geometric window treatments.

Dance Break: The sunporch homeowners like their room so much, they dance The Monkey.

01:21:46.16

Silly Gen!
Gen tries to use pieces of bamboo as accents, but they keep falling apart on her—which causes her to get a serious case of the giggles. Gen later tries to cut down a stalk of bamboo from the homeowners' yard with what looks like a serrated steak knife.

Fashion Report: Dez once again dons a hat during the Designer Chat. This time it's a small black spiky one.

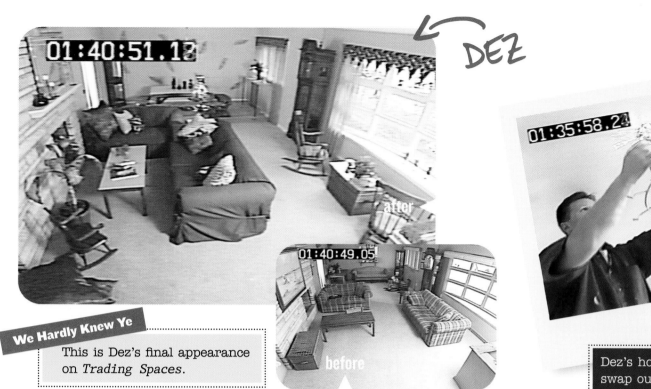

01:40:51.1[?]

DEZ

after

01:40:49.05

before

01:35:58.2[?]

We Hardly Knew Ye

This is Dez's final appearance on *Trading Spaces*.

Dez's homeowners swap out the old light fixture for one that better suits the room's new look.

01:25:38.09

ALEX CAM

Ouch!

As Alex huddles near an outdoor fire to get warm, smoke starts to drift toward her and something gets in her eye. Amy Wynn later roasts marshmallows on the fire.

Tearjerker: The living room wife cries.

Out of Control!

Attempting to shine the sunporch floor, Alex loses control of an electric floor buffer, screams, and falls to the ground.

01:38:11.05

New York: Sherwood Drive

S1
E36

✳ 👹 ♥ | **Cast:** Alex, Doug, Vern, Amy Wynn | **Doug's Room:** ☺ ☺ ☹ | **Vern's Room:** ☺ ☺ ☹

DESIGNED VERN

01:41:33.25

The Rooms

Vern creates a serene bedroom by painting the walls lilac-blue, making a television cabinet out of picture frames, hanging yards of indigo-color velvet, installing sconces containing live beta fish above the bed, and creating a 4-foot-diameter wall clock out of candle sconces and battery-operated clock hands. Doug designs a relaxing Zen-sational bedroom by hanging grass cloth on the walls, making light fixtures out of Malaysian baskets, hanging a full-length mirror on an angle, and building a 6-foot-tall fountain.

01:41:31.29

before

after

Fan Notes
Vern removes his first ceiling fan and replaces it with a five-arm beaded chandelier.

37:58.21

01:02:12.20

Battle of the Sexes
During the opening footage, Amy Wynn beats Doug and Vern at a carnival game and wins a large stuffed animal.

after

DESIGNED BY DOUG

before

Poetic?

Vern's homeowners paint a verse on the wall: "For where your treasure is, there will be your heart."

Can't We All Just Get Along?

Homeowner dissension abounds in this episode! Doug's mother-daughter homeowners tell him that they both have dates and need to stop working at 5 p.m. Doug and Alex explain that the homeowners agreed to complete all the work necessary to redo the room when they signed up for the show. The next morning the homeowners complain to Doug about the hard work they had to do the night before; however, they don't know that Doug stopped by the previous night and found that they had recruited friends to do their homework for them. After a scolding from Doug, the daughter homeowner retorts, "When I get married, I will never pull up carpet, ever!" Doug leaves while the homeowners make faces.

Pump It Up!

Doug's pump isn't strong enough to circulate water through the tall fountain. After much deliberation, he sends Alex off to the store to buy a more powerful pump, which does the trick.

Doug prepares to take a nap outside during Day 2.

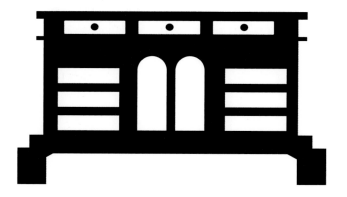

New York: Linda Court

S1
E37

Cast: Alex, Doug, Frank, Amy Wynn   **Doug's Room:** ☺ ☺ ☹ | **Frank's Room:** ☺ ☺ ☹

after

before

The **Rooms**

Doug creates a Mediterranean-flavor living room by covering the walls in yellow Venetian plaster, making custom lamps, building a large armoire to match an existing one, and weaving strips of wood through metal conduit for a woven-wall effect. Frank also heads to the Mediterranean in a living room, applying a faux finish with three shades of yellow paint, then adding stenciled squares on the walls, a faux fresco created from drywall, and gondola-inspired lamps.

DESIGNED BY DOUG

Creative Craftiness: Doug creates a large floor rug by sewing many individual rugs together.

If You Say So
Frank titles his room Mediterranean Trust Me.

Resourceful
Doug's and Frank's designs are so close in concept that Doug sends Alex over to Frank's to borrow some teal and black paint.

after

before

Here's a Pencil ...
Alex nags Frank, saying, "Time is money!" He responds, "Let me write that down so I can embroider that on a whoopee cushion."

Quotable Quotes
Frank's full of fun sayings in this episode! While working on a craft project: "There are no mistakes. There are just embellishment opportunities." On his gondola-inspired lamps: "I just can't leave without some funky little nonsensical nerdy thing like that." On his knickknack choices: "It's a lot like some people. They're just very showy, but they're totally not functional."

DESIGNED BY FRANK

S1	
E38	**New Jersey:** Sam Street

Cast: Alex, Hildi, Laurie, Ty   Hildi's Room: ☺ ☺ ☹ | Laurie's Room: ☺ ☺ ☹

after

before

The Rooms

Laurie warms up a dining room with yellow paint and shades of pink as accents, a custom-built cornice board, and cream paint on the existing furniture. Hildi adds drama and romance to a bedroom by painting the walls an olive-gold, bringing in matching silk fabrics, adding a sofa upholstered in burgundy velvet, extending the existing headboard, and building "pillow pod" seating.

Lucky Laurie

Laurie removes the existing upholstery from the dining room chairs and finds a pretty yellow fabric that matches her design perfectly.

Molding Mishap

Laurie has measurement problems late on Day 2 with a painted, framed fabric display on the wall. The molding Ty cut doesn't fit with what they've already painted, but Laurie solves the problem by tweaking the design.

Notable: Laurie does her best approximation of a Jersey accent.

Budget Booster

Hildi reupholsters a couch she brought with her from Georgia. She keeps pulling coins from the cushions and adding them to her budget.

after

before

> **"** I usually try to find the biggest or the boldest thing that is going to make the most dramatic change. **"**
> —Hildi's design advice

S1
E39

New Jersey: Lincroft

Cast: Alex, Doug, Laurie, Ty

Doug's Room: ☺ 😐 ☹ | Laurie's Room: ☺ 😐 ☹

The Rooms

Doug softens a very red living room by painting the walls sandy taupe, adding wooden strips to accentuate the ceiling height, painting colorful checkerboard designs on coffee tables, sewing several brightly colored rag rugs together to create a large carpet, and designing a wooden candleholder using a rope-and-pulley system. He titles the look Country Kaleidoscope. Laurie adds style and function to a small kitchen by laying parquet vinyl flooring, painting the walls an ocher yellow, wall-mounting the microwave oven, painting the cabinets white, and creating a home office/family message center.

Stress Alert

Doug wants to paint the exposed brick around the wood stove, but his homeowners are against the idea. Frustrated, Doug says to Alex, "Why did we even come here [if they don't want us to change things]?"

Notable

Alex decides that Doug isn't working fast enough, so she takes over his lamp project. She starts talking to the camera about the project but can't get her pliers open. Doug (in the background) starts doing Alex's job, introducing the episode. He mispronounces things. They decide to keep their regular jobs.

Tearjerker: The kitchen homeowners cry.

Fan Ban

Laurie removes a ceiling fan, and in taking it down it falls to the floor and breaks.

¿Cómo?

Laurie and Ty try to assemble a lighting fixture using directions written in Spanish.

66

S1	
E40	

New Jersey: Lafayette Street

Cast: Alex, Frank, Vern, Ty

Frank's Room: ☺ 😐 ☹ | Vern's Room: ☺ 😐 ☹

after

before

Notable: Frank is absolutely unquotable in this episode.

The Rooms

Frank adds Victorian elements to a dining/living room by painting the walls pink with burgundy accents, showcasing the homeowners' collection of wooden houses, applying decorative molding to the existing entertainment center, and creating original wall art using basic woodcarving skills. Vern creates a baby-friendly living room. He paints the walls two shades of sage green, builds a large upholstered ottoman that doubles as a coffee table, builds a sofa out of a mattress, suspends a mantel for the fireplace, and adds bright blue accents.

Baby Love
Vern enlarges pictures of the homeowners' baby and uses them as lampshades on three wall lamps.

Bet Me!
Ty and Alex wager a massage on which designer will finish first. Alex takes Vern, and Ty takes Frank. Both Alex and Ty are underhanded in trying to influence the contest, but Ty eventually wins.

after

before

Swede Thing
Vern attempts to put together an armoire, but the instructions are in Swedish. He convinces Ty to put it together, pointing out that Ty looks more like the man in the illustrations.

Arrivederci: This is Alex's last appearance on *Trading Spaces.*

Season 2

In Season 2, Paige replaces Alex as host, and Dez and Roderick have left the show, leaving 6 designers and 2 carpenters to tackle 90 rooms

6 Designers

$90,000 Total Budget

Celebrities

PaigeCam

Sororities and Fraternities

Spray-Painted Furniture

45 Episodes

1 Host

180 Homeowners

2 Carpenters

Giggle Fits

Nutty the Nutcracker

90 Room Transformations

Quakertown, PA: Quakers Way

S2
E1

 Cast: Paige, Doug, Hildi, Ty

Doug's Room: ☺ ☺ ☹ | Hildi's Room: ☺ ☺ ☹

The Rooms

Hildi introduces viewers to the concept of orthogonal design by painting perpendicular lines on the walls and ceiling of a basement, creating a nine-piece sectional seating area—which she says is her favorite furniture project she's created for *Trading Spaces*—and screening off a large storage area. Doug goes "ball-istic" in a living room, painting the walls lime green, building a custom sofa complete with bowling ball feet, hanging a wall of mirrors, making custom lamps out of gazing balls, and adding brown and blue accents.

after

before

Welcome: This episode is Paige's *Trading Spaces* debut.

The Truth Comes Out

Paige owns up to her dislike of sewing and recounts her experience making a clutch purse in a high school home ec class.

Cute Cart

Hildi carts her lumber from the carpentry area to her room in a little red wagon.

Don't Eat the Artwork!

Although she knows the homeowners have small children, Hildi makes wall art out of acrylic box frames filled with different types of candy.

70

Having a Ball

Doug, Ty, and Paige set a "good" example by grabbing a gazing ball (for Doug's lamp project) from a neighbor's yard. Ty distracts the neighbor, and Doug runs up and takes the gazing ball. Doug tells Paige during Designer Chat that he returned the ball and purchased similar balls to complete his project.

DESIGNED BY DOUG

Notable
The Season 2 premiere introduces the graphic opening credits and the outtakes at the end of the show.

Tuneful
Doug plays the sax, Hildi plays the drums, and Ty plays guitar during the opening segment.

Stress Alert
Doug becomes frustrated while trying to create a decorative piece by wrapping wire around a kick ball. Giving up, he kicks the ball (and the wire) over the fence into a neighbor's yard.

71

S2
E2

New Jersey: Tall Pines Drive

💣 💧 🖌️▪️ | **Cast:** Paige, Laurie, Vern, Amy Wynn | **Laurie's Room:** ☺ 😐 ☹ | **Vern's Room:** ☺ 😐 ☹

The
Rooms

Vern designs a love nest in a bedroom by hanging brown upholstered wall squares, sewing lush draperies using several yards of brown fabric, painting the existing furniture white, installing silver candle chandeliers, and adding new bedside tables. Laurie uses several paint colors in a basement to create a large Matisse-inspired mural. She also makes a chalkboard-top kids' table, installs an art station, creates curtains out of place mats, and hangs louvered panels as a room screen.

after

`01:40:53.1`

`01:44:34.08`

DESIGNED BY VERN

before

Oohs and Aahs

Vern's female homeowner loves his design choices so much that she repeatedly moans as Vern shows her paint and fabric options.

Tearjerker: Both sets of homeowners cry happy tears upon seeing their rooms

" Can I just, like, blink and click my heels and this'll be done? "
—Laurie on her mural project

after

before

DESIGNED BY LAURIE

Notable

A human-size nutcracker named Nutty resides in Laurie's room. Nutty stays in the room during the first half of Day 1, and because one homeowner feels that Nutty is staring at him, he paints over one of Nutty's eyes. Later Nutty floats on a raft in a swimming pool. He makes a final appearance in the passenger seat of a golf cart driven by Amy Wynn.

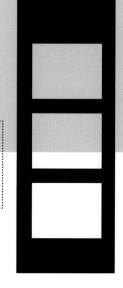

Demolition

In order to transform an existing chest of drawers into an armoire, Laurie and Amy Wynn remove several drawers and demolish the dividers—leaving a large, open space for a television.

S2 E3 Maple Glen, PA: Fiedler Road

✳ | **Cast:** Paige, Genevieve, Laurie, Amy Wynn | Genevieve's Room: ☺ ☺ ☹ | Laurie's Room: ☺ ☺ ☹

The Rooms

Using lilies as inspiration in a living room, Gen paints the walls a yellowed taupe, builds two new couches and a new coffee table, hangs large black-and-white family photos, and pins prints of vintage botanical postcards to the wall. Laurie paints the walls of a bedroom celadon green, creates a headboard from white and yellow silk squares, paints the existing furniture white, installs bamboo pieces as door hardware, and converts bamboo place mats into pillow shams.

Batter Up! Laurie, Gen, and Amy Wynn play softball during B-Roll footage.

Many Moods ...

Laurie repeatedly says she's "in a panic mode" about her room; Gen says she's in a "slo-mo hot zone," meaning that the high room temperature is making her zone out.

Fan-natic

Laurie removes the ceiling fan, and her homeowners protest loudly.

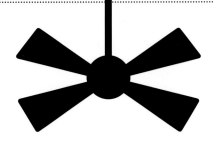

S2 E4 Northampton, PA: James Avenue

Cast: Paige, Frank, Hildi, Ty

Frank's Room: ☺ ☺ ☹ | Hildi's Room: ☺ ☺ ☹

after

before

The Rooms

Hildi updates a living room with mustard-color paint, fuchsia curtains, red tufted pillows, a sisal rug, sunflowers, and a river rock mosaic fireplace. Frank creates a nautical Nantucket theme in a living room by painting the walls pale sage, adding yellow and seafoam green pillows, wrapping rope around the coffee table legs to make the table resemble a pier, and building a dinghy-inspired dog bed.

No Right Turn

Hildi tries to use an industrial sander/scraper, but it won't turn to the right. Things get chaotic as Hildi, Ty, and the male homeowner attempt to get the scraper to work correctly. Eventually Ty runs it in left-hand circles while Hildi and the homeowner run around holding the cord to keep it from wrapping around Ty.

So That's Why

Frank explains his use of found objects in craft projects by saying, "I like giving life to things that would be discarded."

SWITCHEROO

Hildi removes the existing ceiling fan and installs track lighting in its place.

Amen

Frank and his homeowners say a prayer to the "paint gods," thanking them for their color choice.

DESIGNED BY HILDI

DESIGNED BY FRANK

after

before

Yucky Moment

Both sets of homeowners like their rooms, but the homeowners who get the mustard-color living room are concerned that the paint color looks like a dirty diaper.

S2

E5

Providence, RI: Phillips Street

✳ | **Cast:** Paige, Hildi, Vern, Amy Wynn | Hildi's Room: ☺ ☺ ☹ | Vern's Room: ☺ ☺ ☹

The Rooms

Hildi adds sophistication to a living room by painting the walls slate gray, making butter yellow slipcovers, adding a touch of charcoal wax to an existing coffee table and side tables, removing the existing ceiling fan, and replacing the drop ceiling tiles with wood panels. Vern uses the principles of feng shui in a living room by painting the walls and ceiling yellow for wealth, designing a coffee table that holds bamboo stalks for health, attaching small framed mirrors to the ceiling above a candle chandelier, and building a custom fish tank stand for the homeowner's large aquarium.

Ceiling Conflict
Hildi and Amy Wynn disagree on the best way to measure and cut ceiling tiles. Nobody wins.

Conflict Averted
Hildi's homeowners are very worried about her plan to cover the existing furniture with charcoal-color stain and try to talk her out of it. Once Hildi shows them what it looks like, however, they like the look.

Irony, Anyone?
Vern's homeowner breaks a couple ceiling tiles while removing light fixtures. Vern is concerned until he hears that there are extras in the basement. He then jokes that they should just take them all down and the homeowners laugh, blissfully unaware of the ceiling-tile drama upstairs.

Lucky Vern
Vern removes the existing slipcover on the couch and discovers that the original upholstery color is cranberry, which perfectly matches his design.

S2
E6

Providence, RI: Wallis Avenue

 Cast: Paige, Frank, Genevieve, Amy Wynn | Frank's Room: ☺ ☺ ☹ | Genevieve's Room: ☺ ☺ ☹

The Rooms

Frank enlivens a kitchen by using several pastel shades of paint, creating a larger tabletop, laying a vinyl floor, and adding painted chevrons to the cabinets. Gen brings a touch of Tuscany to a bedroom by painting the walls sage green, painting the ceiling yellow, installing floor-to-ceiling shelves, hanging ivy above the headboard, and using light, airy curtains and bed linens.

Quotable Quotes

Frank outdoes his quotable self in this episode. On how long he's been painting: "When God created the world, I was out there painting a fence." On the functionality of his design: "This is real life. This is not page 47." On how much he sweats during Day 1: "I had a kid walk by and throw a coin in my mouth and make a wish."

Stress Alert

When one of Gen's homeowners gives her a great deal of grief over whether or not her design is going to be what their neighbors want, Gen tells her nicely (but firmly) that she's the designer, she's doing what she was brought in to do, and they're going to use her design.

Notable

Frank uses his budget sparingly in order to buy the homeowners a dishwasher (they don't currently have one). When Amy Wynn tells him that she can return two pieces of wood and enable him to buy the appliance, he does a touchdown victory dance. To save installation time, the dishwasher is wheeled in with a bow on the box during The Reveal.

Demolition

Gen and Amy Wynn demolish a built-in desk with rubber mallets and their own feet. Gen is, of course, barefoot.

S2 E7

Boston, MA: Ashfield Street

♥ | **Cast:** Paige, Genevieve, Laurie, Ty   Genevieve's Room: ☺ ☺ ☹ | Laurie's Room: ☺ ☺ ☹

The Rooms

Gen adds a Moroccan touch to a girl's room by painting the walls and ceiling deep blue, installing a large curtained bed, hanging a Moroccan metal lamp, using gold fabric accents, and hanging white draperies. Laurie breathes new life into a bedroom shared by two sisters by painting the walls lavender, creating a trundle bed, painting the existing furniture white, and using ribbons as accents.

after

DESIGNED BY GENEVIEVE

before

Notable
Gen returns the morning of Day 2 to find that her male homeowner (an electrician) has installed two electrical outlets in the freshly painted room. The paint job is messed up, and the homeowner has left insulation and plaster shards all over the floor. When Gen gently confronts him, he stands by his decision.

Happy Ending: The girls who live in Laurie's room like her design so much that they actually turn cartwheels.

Design Dilemma

Laurie thinks she has a serious problem when she discovers the existing wood floors are a pale yellow and not the warm honey color she believed them to be. Ty convinces her that the floor color will still work with her design.

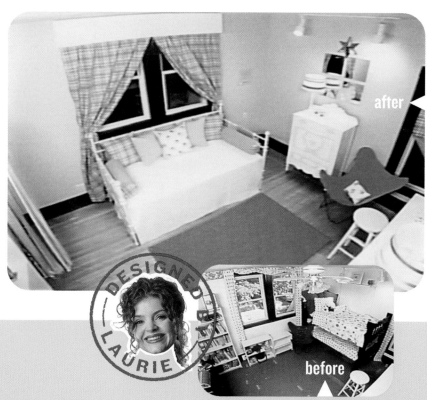

Giggle Fit

Paige drills through a plastic place mat to create a lampshade, but the bit comes out of the drill. When Gen tries to pull the bit out of the place mat, she finds that they've drilled through the homeowners' deck. A huge giggle fit ensues.

S2
E8

Springfield, MA: Sunset Terrace

Cast: Paige, Hildi, Vern, Ty   Hildi's Room: ☺ 😐 ☹ | Vern's Room: ☺ 😐 ☹

The Rooms

Hildi creates a Victorian look in a living room by painting the walls light taupe, using blue and white print fabric for draperies and slipcovers, painting blue stripes on the wood floor, sewing a white faux-fur rug, and transforming one wall with a custom-built Victorian-style fireplace with a marble surround. Vern goes for an even more Victorian look in the other living room by painting the walls yellow to highlight the homeowners' French provincial furniture, laying a Victorian rug, making a light fixture with silver mesh and hand-strung beads, and creating a custom art piece using celestial and fleur-de-lis stencils.

Demolition
Hildi and Ty demolish the existing mantel to make room for Hildi's Victorian mantel addition.

Time Well Spent
Vern gets concerned that he won't have enough time for his design projects because Ty spends so much time working with Hildi on Day 1. Vern manages to finish his room (with all projects complete) on time.

S2
E9

Boston, MA: Institute Road

Cast: Paige, Doug, Frank, Ty

Doug's Room: ☺ ☺ ☹ | Frank's Room: ☺ ☺ ☹

01:40:41.23 after

DESIGNED BY DOUG

01:40:40.02 before

The Rooms

Doug looks to the leaves for inspiration in his Autumnal Bliss bedroom. He covers the walls with bark paper, upholsters the headboard in linen, hangs yellow linen draperies, and frames fall leaves as art. Frank creates a Shakespearean library by painting the walls red, hand-painting Elizabethan musician cutouts for the walls, and painting a rounded stone pattern on the floor.

Traveling Companions

Doug goes to find autumn leaves with Paige and Ty. Doug drives a golf cart, Paige sits on the back, and Ty rides on a skateboard by holding on to a string tied to the back of the cart.

DESIGNED BY FRANK

Not Listening

Doug tries to explain his leaf art project to Paige, who keeps jumping on a trampoline in the background and saying, "Yeah, yeah, yeah," pretending as though she is listening.

01:39:47.00 after

01:39:44.08 before

Quotable Quotes

Frank's full of great quotes in this episode. On what may be under the carpet he's ripping up: "It could be the gates of heaven or the portals of hell." On what the carpet is saying to them: "I'm going to mold you to death." On how much he loves his use of red paint: "Throw me on the ground and make me write a bad check."

Fashion Report

Paige wears a brown top with poofy Elizabethan-style sleeves in honor of the homeowners' love of Shakespeare.

Homework Time

Ah, homework ...

The word conjures memories of late nights and caffeinated soda—often spent hunched over a notebook or computer keyboard. But, this is homework *Trading Spaces* style, where the designer gives his or her homeowners assignments to complete on the night of Day 1. No, the homeowners won't get rapped on the knuckles if they don't finish—and they won't be graded—but if they don't finish on time, it can mean disaster on Day 2, not to mention a disappointed designer. Here are some of the most memorable homework assignments and early morning Day 2 events.

Pass the Bubbly!

Frank's homeowners don't finish their homework, claiming a neighbor came over with champagne. (Key West, FL: Elizabeth Street, Season I, Episode 23)

The Never-Ending Project

Vern and his team got virtually no sleep between Days I and 2, because they were constructing a built-in storage unit. (Philadelphia, PA: Gettysburg Lane, Season 3, Episode 9)

Isn't That Sweet ...

Day I is Frank's homeowners' anniversary. The husband has flowers delivered to his wife, and Frank stays to do their homework that night so they can go out and celebrate. (Austin, TX: Birdhouse Drive, Season I, Episode 26)

Homework Headaches

On Day I, Doug's homeowners (a mother-daughter team) tell him that they both have dates that night because they thought they stopped working on the room at 5. Doug and Alex try to explain to them—repeatedly—that they agreed to do the work necessary to redo the room when they signed up for the show. The next morning, the homeowners complain to Doug about all the hard work they did the night before. They don't know that he stopped by that night and discovered they had recruited friends to come and do their homework for them. Doug scolds them, the homeowners make faces, and Doug walks away. (New York: Sherwood Drive, Season I, Episode 36)

Break Time

On the morning of Day 2, Kia and her homeowners are in robes, drinking coffee because they're so tired. Hildi finds her team the morning of Day 2 with a large photo of one of the other homeowners, which they're using for "inspiration." (Pennsylvania: Cresheim Road, Season 3, Episode 59)

Thanks, Frank!

Frank's female homeowner was recently in an accident and has difficulty with soreness in her neck and shoulders. As a result, Frank tells her to go rest and he'll stay and do her homework. Frank puts on her *Trading Spaces* smock and impersonates his homeowner, saying, "I can't believe that little, fat, rotund twerp gave us all this homework after we worked all that time." (New Jersey: Manitoba Trail, Season 3, Episode 13)

No Time for Faux

Laurie gives her homeowners the job of painting a headboard for one of their homework assignments. When Laurie arrives the morning of Day 2, they are just starting to prime it. She is upset because she wanted to put a faux finish on it and can't because the paint won't be dry in time. Paige does an extended PaigeCam interview with Laurie, who talks about not understanding why they didn't do it. At the end of it she says, "I'm just so confused." (Maine: Joseph Drive, Season 3, Episode 3)

Go Figure

Actor Beverly Mitchell had forbidden the other team—actors Jeff and George Stoltz—to sleep in her bedroom the night of Day 1, afraid of what they might do to it. They did it anyway. Paige and Edward discover the two there the morning of Day 2 with plates of sausages and dog food, Beverly's Nickelodeon Teen Choice awards, and trash strewn all over her bed. They take several Polaroids of themselves doing things to mess up her bedroom that are eventually displayed in the finished room. (Los Angeles, CA: Seventh Street, Season 3, Episode 52)

Philadelphia, PA: Jeannes Street

S2 E10

Cast: Paige, Genevieve, Vern, Amy Wynn   Genevieve's Room: ☺ ☺ ☹   Vern's Room: ☺ ☺ ☹

The Rooms

Gen turns a basement den into a 3-D Scrabble board by painting taupe and white grids on the floors and ceiling, installing a black wall-length bar, making pillows that mimic Scrabble board squares, and framing game boards to hang on the wall. Vern uses the female homeowner's love of the holiday season for inspiration in a living room by painting the walls and ceiling deep red, making camel-color slipcovers and draperies, and building a dark wood armoire with mirrored doors.

TIME TEST

Vern's male homeowner has difficulty wrapping lights around two mini pine trees. There are several hurry-up shots of him trying to figure out the best way to do it.

Maybe Next Time

Vern's female homeowner gives him grief about painting the ceiling. She also wants to build radiator covers. Vern draws up plans to do so, but Amy Wynn can't complete the work in time. The homeowner is unhappy about it.

Giggle Fit

Gen and Paige try to screw lazy Susan tops to bar stools. First, Gen's screws aren't long enough; then, they can't get the screws in, and Gen realizes she has the drill in reverse. Next, their screws are too long, and the tops won't swivel. A huge giggle fit ensues.

New Jersey: Perth Road

Cast: Paige, Frank, Laurie, Amy Wynn   **Frank's Room:** ☺ ☺ ☹   **Laurie's Room:** ☺ ☺ ☹

The Rooms

Frank gives a living room a homier feel by adding light camel paint, a coffee table topped with a picture frame, textured folk art on the wall, and a custom-built armoire (he says, "It's kind of a puppet theater cathedral"). Laurie redecorates a bedroom without altering the existing Queen Anne furniture. She paints the walls a warm apricot, builds a custom canopy that rests on top of the four-poster bed, and adds bookshelves as nightstands.

Boys Club

Frank's male homeowner complains about having to sew because he doesn't think it's a manly activity. He immediately points out that he's secure in his manhood. Frank retorts, "Well, then if you're so damned secure, start putting that stuffing in that pillow."

Count the Candles

It's one of the homeowner's birthdays, and he's presented with a cake by his neighbors after both Reveals.

Making Do

Laurie jokes she is "freaking out" because her swing-arm lamps haven't arrived by the morning of Day 2. She tells Paige that she has called to track the package, but the tracking wasn't helpful. She then waits on the street looking for the delivery truck. The lamps never arrive, and she has to substitute discount store fixtures.

Notable

Laurie's female homeowner is a former Philadelphia Eagles cheerleader.

85

S2 E12

Maryland: Village Green

Cast: Paige, Doug, Genevieve, Amy Wynn   **Doug's Room:** ☺ ☺ ☹ | **Genevieve's Room:** ☺ ☺ ☹

after

before

The Rooms

Gen refines a bedroom by painting one wall chocolate brown, covering the ceiling with gold-metallic paint, installing a custom geometric shelving unit, making a fountain, decoupaging sewing patterns to a wall, and creating a light fixture out of a large wicker ball. Doug creates an elegant and sophisticated look in a bedroom by painting the walls gray, building a large upholstered headboard with storage in the back, painting the furniture white, and painting large Matisse-inspired figures directly on the wall.

DESIGNED BY GENEVIEVE

Giggle Fit

To create custom lampshades, Gen wraps rounded glass vases with plastic wrap and then winds glued string around them à la papier-mâché. Once the vases are dry, Gen and Paige put on safety glasses and start hammering the shades to break the vases on the inside. Gen thinks her idea of including the plastic wrap will keep them from having to touch any shards of glass. She's wrong. After a huge giggle fit, Gen looks into the camera and warns, "This project isn't for kids."

Fashion Report: Gen wears two braids in her hair.

after

before

DESIGNED BY DOUG

Reveal-ing Moment

The gray bedroom homeowners love their room, but the brown bedroom homeowners don't like theirs. In fact, the female homeowner doesn't like anything but the fountain and says that the sewing patterns will go the next day.

Name Game

Doug titles his room Strip Stripe for the gray and white striped fabric he uses to cover the headboard.

Doug traces figures onto the wall with the help of an overhead projector (left). Gen and her female homeowner decoupage sewing patterns to a wall (middle). Amy Wynn poses with a frame she constructed for Doug's custom artwork (right).

Reveal-ing Moment, Part 2

During the end credits, Amy Wynn is embarrassed when she's caught applying lip balm, and the female brown bedroom homeowner tells the cameraman she's "had enough" and walks out of the room.

TX E100S 19 TX E100S 20

18A 18 19A 19 20A 20

S2 E13 **Maryland:** Fairway Court

Cast: Paige, Doug, Vern, Amy Wynn   **Doug's Room:** ☺ ☺ ☹   **Vern's Room:** ☺ ☺ ☹

The Rooms

Vern softens a bedroom by painting the walls a light gray, hanging charcoal draperies, suspending a canopy over the existing sleigh bed, and dangling 100 clear crystals from the canopy edge. Doug designs a fantasy bedroom suite for train enthusiasts by rounding the ceiling edges, covering the walls with blue paint and fabric, and building fake walls and windows to mimic the inside of a Pullman car.

after

before

DESIGNED BY VERN

DESIGNED BY DOUG

after

Fashion Report: Doug's hair is super slicked back.

before

Quotable Quote
Vern states during Designer Chat, "Precision doesn't have to go overtime; you just have to be well planned."

Notable
Doug claims that this design is the biggest challenge he's taken on in a *Trading Spaces* episode. Paige refers to it as a "marvelous achievement."

Chicago, IL: Edward Road

S2
E14

Cast: Paige, Frank, Laurie, Ty

Frank's Room: ☺ ☺ ☹ | Laurie's Room: ☺ ☺ ☹

after

before

DESIGNED BY FRANK

Quotable Quote

At the end of Day 1, Frank says, "I'm gonna go home, have a pedicure, manicure, shower, have my designer stylist come in, and ... I'll see you in the morning."

The Rooms

Frank adds an aged copper look to a kitchen by using touches of terra-cotta, copper, and green paint. He also lays earth-tone vinyl flooring, paints a faux-tile backsplash, makes a large floorcloth, and adds a butcher-block island. Laurie gives a living room a touch of European flair by painting a faux-fresco finish in yellow tones, installing dark wooden beams on the ceiling, hanging burlap draperies, painting a faux-inlay top on an occasional table, and repeating an X motif throughout the room.

We're Counting!

Frank asks about the "heiny quotient" for the third time in the series. This time it's for an upholstered bench he plans to add to the room.

You're Outta Here!

Laurie's male homeowner is a (self-admitted) very, very bad painter and is banished from the room while it is being painted.

after

before

DESIGNED BY LAURIE

Laurie's Design Theory

"I want to give them a room that is a basic skeleton with beautiful walls, the layout the way I think it needs to be ... and then, hopefully, what I trigger them to do ... [is get] a new love seat."

S2
E15

Chicago, IL: Spaulding Avenue

Cast: Paige, Doug, Hildi, Ty

Doug's Room: ☺ ☺ ☹ | Hildi's Room: ☺ ☺ ☹

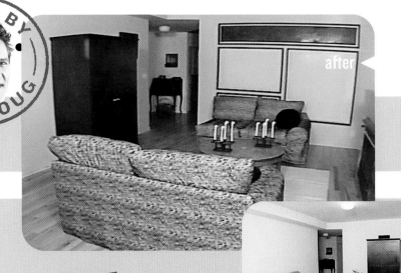
after

The Rooms

DESIGNED BY DOUG

Doug adds a little funk to a living room by painting the walls yellow, using Venetian plaster to make black and yellow blocks on a wall, upholstering the furniture with zebra-print fabric, and suspending a tabletop from the ceiling to create a dining area. Hildi brings the outdoors into a bedroom. She paints the walls cream and the trim a deep plum, and then she draws large "swooshes" of grass on the walls with chalk pastels. She adds a row of grass planter boxes along one wall, uses bursts of orange in pillows, and makes a large wooden bed.

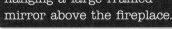
Bold Idea

Doug announces that he's going to take a "risk" by hanging a large framed mirror above the fireplace.

before

Conflict

Doug wants to glaze a 2-inch border around the wood floor. He paints a small strip to show what it will look like, and the homeowners veto it. Doug, feigning disappointment, wipes it off.

Big Spender
Hildi admits that the wood for her bed and bench totaled $700—70 percent of her budget.

after

before

DESIGNED BY HILDI

Sticky Situation
After drawing grass blades with chalk pastel on the wall, Hildi and her homeowners seal the drawings with several cans of hair spray.

Problem Solved!
Ty can't get Hildi's window bench into the bedroom. He eventually has to remove the center legs to get it inside the door.

PAIGE CAM

S2 E16

Chicago, IL: Fairview Avenue

Cast: Paige, Genevieve, Vern, Ty | Genevieve's Room: ☺ ☺ ☹ | Vern's Room: ☺ ☺ ☹

The Rooms

Vern brightens a kitchen by painting the walls pear green, painting the cabinets white, creating a new cabinet for storage, making a new table, laying a black and white geometric rug, upholstering a storage bench that doubles as seating at the table, and hanging upholstered cushions against the wall above the bench. Gen gives the lodge look to a basement living room by painting the walls cinnamon, installing a pine plank ceiling, hanging wood wainscoting, slipcovering the furniture, and highlighting the fireplace with built-in shelves.

DESIGNED BY VERN

Vern and Paige measure concentric squares for the tabletop design (left). Vern removes peel-and-stick vinyl floor tiles from the backsplash (right).

Notable
Paige and Gen agree during Designer Chat that out of all the rooms she's designed on the show, the living room Gen designed here is most like her own personal style.

after

before

DESIGNED BY GENEVIE

• •

Silly Gen!

Gen tries to dye white fabric orange to use as slipcovers. She and her female homeowner spend a great deal of time working on this project, but the fabric comes out pink.

Rest Time
Ty tries to take a break on an empty school bus, and Gen has to drag him back to work.

Heel Help: Gen breaks the heel of her boot and goes to Ty for the repair.

S2 E17

Colorado: Berry Avenue

⑦ ⑤ | **Cast:** Paige, Genevieve, Hildi, Amy Wynn | Genevieve's Room: ☺ ☺ ☹ | Hildi's Room: ☺ ☺ ☹

after

before

DESIGNED BY GENEVIEVE

The Rooms

Gen paints the walls of a kitchen bright eggplant, paints the cabinets vanilla-sage, removes the center panels of the cabinet doors to showcase the dishes inside, and prints each family member's face on a chair cover for personalized seating. Hildi creates an intimate living room by painting the walls a deep chocolate brown, using sage fabrics, transforming the coffee table into a large ottoman, and installing a wall-size fountain to create the illusion of a third window.

Joke Time

Gen's homeowners rent a jackhammer and use it in a bucket of hardened concrete to make their neighbors think their floor is being ripped out.

All Choked Up

Gen explains her color choices by tearing apart a boiled artichoke. Paige later enters the room and mistakenly pops the bitter heart into her mouth. She quickly spits it out.

Technical Stuff

Gen attempts to explain how she uses her laptop to reproduce the family photos for the chair covers. Paige asks several questions, but Gen isn't really able to answer them. Gen describes the computer program she's using as a "special program for a special girl."

Resourceful: Gen sketches her table design—including measurements—on Amy Wynn's palm.

Great Taste

Hildi brushes melted chocolate on the wall as her homeowners enter at the beginning of the show. She then paints the wall with the chocolate brown paint that they'll be using.

DESIGNED BY HILDI

Silly Stuff

During Designer Chat, Paige and Gen wear the chair covers with the homeowners' faces over their heads and role-play the homeowners' reaction to their new room.

before

Water Woes

Hildi and Paige cover the bottom of a plastic window box planter with silicone to seal it. When they try to set a large piece of glass in the box to create the fountain, Paige cuts through the silicone, breaking the seal. Water quickly seeps across the wood floor. (After cleaning up the mess, Hildi decides to use two layers of pond lining to seal the planter.)

Budget Buster: Hildi's lush living room design puts her over budget.

Joke Time, Part 2

In an attempt to get back at Gen's team for using the jackhammer, Hildi's homeowners remove the music rack from the family's cherished piano and have Paige take it to Amy Wynn and discuss ways to fix it in front of one of Gen's homeowners.

S2 E18 | Colorado: Cherry Street

☺ ? | **Cast:** Paige, Genevieve, Laurie, Amy Wynn | Genevieve's Room: ☺ ☺ ☹ | Laurie's Room: ☺ ☺ ☹

The Rooms

Gen gives a living room a punch of personality by painting the walls brick red with sage accents, hanging antlers on the walls, installing floor-to-ceiling shelving, making a focal point out of one of the homeowners' landscape photos, and creating an inlaid rug. Laurie applies a touch of mod to a living room by painting gray and yellow horizontal stripes on the walls, building a new glass-top coffee table, hanging silver silk draperies, and adding a piece of custom artwork.

after

before

"If this were a country, it would be Beigeland."

—Gen describes her room's look prior to redecorating

Carpet Cut-Ups

Rather than lay a green rug on top of the beige carpet, Gen cuts out a patch of the carpet and lays the new rug inside. Gen warns viewers, "Don't do this if you're renting." Amy Wynn walks by while they're cutting the carpeting and says under her breath, "Wow. That's scary looking."

¡Me Gusta!

Gen says she bought the extra antlers for her design from a woman selling them on the side of the street in Mexico.

Time Crunch

Laurie spends most of Day 1 laying out tape to form the horizontal paint lines. She also has several plans to add storage to the room, but there is not enough time or wood to make her plans a reality.

after

before

DESIGNED BY LAURIE

Stress Alert

Laurie, Paige, and Laurie's homeowner voice differing opinions on how to hang a large abstract canvas. Laurie finally tells them to hang it her way because "I'm the designer."

Amy Wynn and Paige are attacked by tumbleweeds.

S2
E19

Colorado: Andes Way

💧 | **Cast:** Paige, Frank, Vern, Amy Wynn

Frank's Room: ☺ 😐 ☹ | Vern's Room: ☺ 😐 ☹

after

before

The
Rooms

Frank creates a family-friendly living room by rag-rolling the walls with cream and peach paint, hanging valances coated with brown builder's paper, building a white and sage armoire, and creating a kids' nook with a large art table, plant murals on the walls, and wooden clouds nailed to the ceiling. Vern stripes a living room, laying two colors of laminate flooring in alternating rows, painting a red horizontal stripe on the khaki walls, and continuing the same stripe across the draperies.

> ## "It's kinda, like, goth-eyed wonky.
> —Frank, describing his paint technique

after

before

Notable

Amy Wynn participates in Frank's crafts project, helping him cover the valance with builder's paper. She gives up after forgetting to apply crafts glue when trying to adhere the paper. Frank calls her a "craft wimp."

Tearjerker
The female family room homeowner cries tears of happiness.

Smart Spender
Instead of buying the cording specifically for building lamps, Vern saves money by buying an extension cord and cutting off the nonplug end.

S2
E20

Colorado: Stoneflower Drive

💣 ✖ | **Cast:** Paige, Doug, Frank, Amy Wynn   **Doug's Room:** ☺ 😐 ☹ | **Frank's Room:** ☺ 😐 ☹

after

before

Dog Decor

Frank justifies his dog bed design by saying, "Try and get the feeling of what it would be like if you were a dog and you were lying in your bed going, 'I need a little wall decor here.'"

Demolition
Amy Wynn and Doug destroy the wood railing between the kitchen and the living room.

The Rooms

Frank injects some whimsy into a bedroom by painting the walls celadon green, building a large headboard that mimics a skyline, creating a matching dog bed, and hanging gold curtains. Doug updates a living room with a design he calls Smoke Screen. He paints the walls moss green, removes colonial molding, adds pewter accents, hangs pleated metal screening, and builds screen doors to cover shelving around the fireplace.

Gotcha!
Frank brings in tacky dolphin pillows, and the female homeowner says that she loves them. Frank laughs and explains that he's only using them as inexpensive pillow forms.

• • • • • • • • • • • • • • • • • •

Helping Out
Doug lounges in a deck chair drinking iced tea while reading faux-finish directions to his homeowners. He tosses them supplies instead of getting up.

after

Welcome to the Club: Doug removes his first ceiling fan.

before

Seattle, WA: 137th Street

S2
E21

💧 👀 ♥ | **Cast:** Paige, Doug, Frank, Ty | **Doug's Room:** ☺ ☺ ☹ | **Frank's Room:** ☺ ☺ ☹

after

before

The Rooms

Doug does Denim Deluxe in a living room. He paints a white grid pattern on chocolate walls, slipcovers the furniture with brown and ivory denim, makes art pieces with brightly colored tissue paper, lowers the existing coffee table, installs white wainscoting, and builds a white facade to cover the brick fireplace. Frank brightens a living room by painting the walls reddish orange and yellow, installing a new mantel, hanging shelves on either side of the fireplace, making a fireplace screen painted with folk art characters, and creating a window valance with place mats and clothespins.

Fashion Report: Doug sports a denim jacket with the collar turned up.

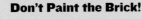

Don't Paint the Brick!

The living room homeowners leave Doug strict instructions not to paint their fireplace, but Doug wants to paint it white. His homeowners repeatedly argue with him about it. When Doug states that he's not happy, one of his homeowners turns ultrapositive and says, "It's OK not to be happy sometimes!" She suggests covering the fireplace with fabric, noting "You guys love cloth!" When Doug leaves the room in frustration, she looks to the camera and says, "Well, now he's a little cranky."

Reveal-ing Moments

A classic Reveal that must be seen to be believed! The denim living room homeowners are disappointed with their room (the male homeowner surmises Doug's design as "I see a lot of firewood"), and the female homeowner leaves the room in tears while her microphone continues running. The episode has a somewhat happy ending, with the male homeowner noting that "at least the room isn't orthogonal [like one of Hildi's infamous designs]."

> ## This may be my shining moment.
> —Doug on his idea to slipcover the fireplace rather than paint it

Frank teaches his male homeowner the finer points of decorative painting.

before

after

DESIGNED BY FRANK

Huh?

Frank describes what he wants to paint on the walls by saying, "We're going to be doing a kind of rectangular, kind of checky, not really country, not really contemporary, just homey, cottagey, but with a kind of a more upbeat level."

S2 E22 — **Seattle, WA:** Dakota Street

$ | **Cast:** Paige, Laurie, Vern, Ty | Laurie's Room: ☺ ☺ ☹ | Vern's Room: ☺ ☺ ☹

The Rooms

Vern adds drama and romance to a living room by painting the walls golden yellow, hanging brown draperies, building an armoire with red upholstered door panels, slipcovering the furniture in white fabric dyed with tea bags, and constructing red candle torchères. Laurie tries to convince her homeowners that she can warm up a bedroom with parchment-color paint, soft white and blue fabrics, various chocolate brown accents on the furniture and headboard, and painted partition screens.

DESIGNED BY VERN

before

after

Move Over, Ty ...

When Ty doesn't have time to make Vern's upholstered armoire doors, Vern and the male homeowner go out to the shop to make the pieces by themselves.

Ty takes a break in the shop.

Pass the Tartar Sauce

Paige catches a large fish while standing in a fish market during the introduction.

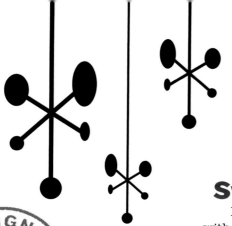

Sweet Dreams?

Laurie becomes frustrated with the headboard frame and exclaims, "This is a nightmare!"

I01:37:51.05

I40:23.21

after

Crafty Cover-Up

While building Laurie's room partitions on Day 2, Ty accidentally nails into the freshly painted walls because the nails are too long. Laurie stands in the middle of the room with her hands on her head and says nothing. She eventually decides to try to cover many of the holes with large framed family photographs.

I01:40:21.20

before

Reveal-ing Moment

Both of the female homeowners dislike their rooms. In fact, the bedroom homeowner keeps talking about all the work she'll have to do the next day to change it.

I01:46:29.10

Budget Buster

Laurie ends up $5.53 over budget.

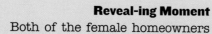

Sew What? Vern's male homeowner sits down at the sewing machine and is confused about how to "make it go."

S2
E23

Seattle, WA: 56th Place

Cast: Paige, Genevieve, Hildi, Ty | Genevieve's Room: ☺ ☺ ☹ | Hildi's Room: ☺ ☺ ☹

The
Rooms

Hildi turns a basement rec room into a tent, covering it in magenta and taupe fabric hung from the ceiling. She also brings in new coffee and side tables and slipcovers new sofas with magenta fabric (when the freshly painted existing sofas are ruined after being left overnight in the rain). Gen creates an Asian living room, using shimmery silver and red paints and coating one wall in a metal paint that oxidizes to a rusted finish. She makes a valance out of an obi and uses cedar flowerpots as picture frames.

Furniture Follies

Hildi surprises her homeowners by spray-painting the existing upholstered furniture magenta. Later one of Hildi's homeowners brings Paige in with her eyes closed and then reveals the painted furniture. Paige is shocked and says, "This looks pretty bad."

Budget Crisis

Hildi arrives on Day 2 to find that the tarp blew off the freshly painted furniture; the furniture has been rained on and ruined. Paige eventually agrees to break the rules, letting Hildi go severely over budget in order to buy new furniture. Hildi leaves and returns with two new slipcovered sofas (total cost: $500).

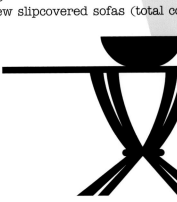

Have Coffee, Will Travel
Gen's homeowners arrive carrying their own espresso maker.

Paige and Gen's female homeowner shop for supplies late in Day 1.

after

Conflict
Gen meets opposition when she reveals her Asian theme to her homeowners. They state that their neighbors hate Asian decor, but Gen decides to go ahead with her plans.

Tearjerker: The female rust wall living room homeowner cries.

before

Them's the Breaks

While Gen and Paige are crafting a lamp, they recount all of the bad things that have happened when they work on projects together. While lamenting all the things they've broken, Paige slips with the glass globe she's cleaning and breaks it. Gen states, "This is a show of human errors."

S2
E24

Oregon: Alyssum Avenue

? —¦ | **Cast:** Paige, Genevieve, Hildi, Amy Wynn | Genevieve's Room: ☺ 😐 ☹ | Hildi's Room: ☺ 😐 ☹

The Rooms

Hildi creates a cozy bedroom by upholstering the walls and ceiling with light blue fabric, building a four-poster bed frame, draping sheer patterned fabric from the ceiling center over the bed corners, hanging a chandelier above the bed, and adding a blue monogram to white bed linens. Gen adds a graphic touch to a living room by painting the walls bright yellow, covering a wall with 6-inch wooden squares, building cedar shelving under the stairs, and hanging clotheslines to display art and photos.

after

before

Girl Power

Hildi's female homeowner learns how to use the nail gun and is afraid of hurting Amy Wynn with it.

after

Hip to Be Square

Gen's wall of squares requires numerous steps. The design calls for more than a thousand squares of wood, all of which must be specially cut; each square has to be stacked on top of others to create different heights; and the stacked squares must be glued together, stapled to reinforce the glue, primed, painted, hung on the wall, and puttied over to cover the nail holes.

Magic!

Hildi transforms two outdoor wicker chairs into upholstered indoor chairs.

before

Wonder Woman

Hildi runs into problems when her bed design isn't very stable. Amy Wynn makes a few structural adjustments and stabilizes it.

Oregon: Alsea Court

💣 $ | **Cast:** Paige, Frank, Laurie, Amy Wynn | Frank's Room: ☺ 😐 ☹ | Laurie's Room: ☺ 😐 ☹

after

before

The Rooms

Frank goes south of the border in a kitchen by painting a serape on the ceiling, making a basket-weave wall treatment with sheet metal strips, painting the cabinet door center panels silver, designing a distressed tabletop, and upholstering dining chairs with serape fabric. Laurie brings warmth to a living room by painting the walls amber, using several expensive fabrics in warm harvest shades, building an entertainment center with gold filigree door insets, and designing a large central ottoman.

SIGNED BY FRANK

Demolition
Frank, Amy Wynn, Paige, and Frank's homeowners demolish an entire row of kitchen cabinets in order to open up the room.

> " I feel very Carmen Miranda-ish. Now, quick, get me a pineapple drink and a funny hat. —Frank "

Time Out

Frank's homeowners question most of his decisions. After fighting to nix a wall decoration late on Day 2, Frank hits a breaking point and says, "I'm going to go fix myself a beverage. You can put those anywhere you want to. The suggestions are numerous, but I won't get into them right now."

Budget Crisis
When Laurie returns the morning of Day 2, she finds that she has run out of brown paint. She still needs to paint the ottoman and finish painting the armoire, but she's out of money. She says, "I'm really kinda stressed about this." In the end, Laurie winds up over budget.

before

after

DESIGNED BY LAURIE

Portland, OR: Everett Street

S2 E26

Cast: Paige, Doug, Vern, Amy Wynn

Doug's Room: ☺ ☺ ☹ | **Vern's Room:** ☺ ☺ ☹

The Rooms

Doug transforms a family room into an Art Deco theater by painting the floors and ceiling chocolate brown, covering the walls with chocolate brown fabric, building graduated platforms for silver chairs, suspending the television from the ceiling, and installing aisle lights. Vern creates a cohesive look in a living/dining room by painting the walls sage green and hanging sage draperies with white satin stripes on the windows and the walls of the dining area. He also builds a custom armoire and buffet with square wooden insets stained various colors and creates a custom lampshade with handmade art paper.

after

Fashion Report: Doug wears a knit skullcap.

Not in My House!
One of Doug's fabrics is incredibly musty, and he admits that the smell is so strong he wouldn't use it in his own house.

before

Stress Alert

Doug's homeowners continually question whether there will be room for a computer in the finished design. By the morning of Day 2, Doug is weary of fending them off and mixes a glass of antacid. One of the homeowners again asks him where the computer is going, and Doug points out, rather forcefully, that it will stay in the room.

▼01:39:16.08

after

DESIGNED BY VERN

Guy Thing
Vern explains stuffing a pillow and mounting a wall sconce to his male homeowner by relating these processes to taxidermy, the homeowner's hobby.

▼01:39:13.22

before

▼01:35:05.26

Vern and his homeowners sort the stained insets for the custom armoire.

:55.12

Tearjerker: The sage living room homeowner laughs very hard upon seeing her room, then cries tears of joy.

S2 E27

Santa Clara, CA: Lafayette Street

🎓 💲 ⊣▮ | **Cast:** Paige, Frank, Laurie, Ty | **Frank's Room:** ☺ 😐 ☹ | **Laurie's Room:** ☺ 😐 ☹

The Rooms

Frank adds a festive touch to the living room of a Delta Gamma residence by painting the walls two shades of a peachy orange; highlighting the curved ceiling with stenciled stars, triangles, swirls, and dots; painting the sorority letters above the fireplace; and installing a window bench seat. Laurie updates the Delta Gamma chapter room by painting the walls a muted seafoam, stenciling yellow anchors on the walls, designing a coffee table with hidden additional seating, and making a candelabra from a captain's wheel.

Paint Fun
Frank reveals the wall colors by having both the sorority sisters close their eyes, dip their hands in the paint, and then smear it on the wall.

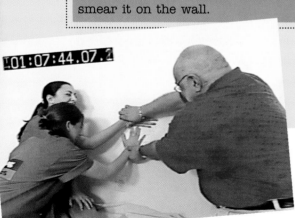

Huh?
Frank describes the ceiling paint technique by saying, "That will give that hand-painted, kind of European slash Mediterranean slash boutique hotel look."

after

before

Adoration
During a bumper shot, fans sitting outside on the street hold a large sign that reads, "Frank is the cat's meow."

Word Lesson
While crafting with his sorority team, Frank says "cattywampus," and they question him about whether he made up the word.

after

before

Acting!

Paige pretends to be a surprised sorority sister at the last Reveal and starts screaming and hugging the sorority members.

Go, Girl

Laurie reminisces about her sorority days as a Kappa and talks about having to dress up like Carmen Miranda and sing Kappa, Kappa-Cabana to the tune of Barry Manilow's "Copacabana."

Notable

Frank does a cartwheel during the sped-up footage of his team removing furniture from his room.

Budget Buster

Over budget by 11 cents, Laurie presents Paige with that amount during Designer Chat.

S2
E28

California: Corte Rosa

$ ◊ | **Cast:** Paige, Laurie, Vern, Ty   Laurie's Room: ☺ ☺ ☹ | Vern's Room: ☺ ☺ ☹

The Rooms

Vern gives a bedroom an exotic resort decor by painting the walls light chino, upholstering the bedside tabletops with faux leather, adding tribal- and safari-print fabrics to the draperies and bed linens, hanging a red glass light fixture, and building storage cabinets on a large plant ledge. Laurie creates romance in a bedroom by painting the walls sage green, hanging a French tester canopy above the bed, painting the existing furniture mocha brown, installing a window seat with storage cabinets, and hanging dark green draperies.

Tearjerker: One of the sage bedroom homeowners cries.

SIGNED BY VERN

⌐01:40:01.07

after

⌐01:39:55.28

before

"**If this doesn't produce a third child, this is gonna be a total failure.**"
—Vern, commenting on the desired effect of his design

For Fun

Vern, Laurie, and Ty pedal tiny three-wheeled bikes at the start of the show.

⌐01:39:54.28
after

DESIGNED BY LAURIE

Budget Buster

Laurie's lush bedroom sets her back more than $1,000.

Notable
Typically mellow Ty is stressed much of the episode because of his workload and falls behind on his carpentry work.

⌐01:39:50.29

before

California: Grenadine Way

S2 E29

✳ $ | **Cast:** Paige, Frank, Vern, Ty | Frank's Room: ☺ ☺ ☹ | Vern's Room: ☺ ☺ ☹

after

before

The Rooms

Vern looks to vintage Indian fabrics for inspiration in a bedroom. He paints the walls soft blue, lays wood laminate flooring, installs a large headboard of basket-woven iridescent fabric, and hangs amber glass candleholders. Frank gives ethnic flair to a living room by painting a mantel with stripes of mustard, white, taupe, and black; designing a large wooden sculpture; and building a new coffee table, armoire, and cornice box.

DESIGNED BY VERN

Headboard Heaches

While constructing the large headboard, Vern's team accidentally nails it to the newly installed laminate flooring.

Budget Buster

Vern is over budget by $2.47.

before

DESIGNED BY FRANK

Get Well!
Vern has laryngitis and is often barely able to speak. He tells Ty on Day 1 that he's doing his best Darth Vader impersonation. By the morning of Day 2, he has to communicate with his homeowners by writing on pieces of paper.

after

Design by Committee
Frank's homeowners question most of his decisions, and he adapts most aspects of his design as a result.

> **I'm puffed.**
> —Frank, after finding out he is under budget

Fan Ban: Vern removes the existing ceiling fan.

Berkeley, CA: Prospect Street

S2
E30

👐 🔨 🎓 $ ♥ | **Cast:** Paige, Doug, Genevieve, Ty | Doug's Room: ☺ 😐 ☹ | Genevieve's Room: ☺ 😐 ☹

The Rooms

Doug cleans up the Delta Upsilon fraternity chapter room (and goes DU-clectic) by painting the walls lime green, installing bench seating, constructing two huge circular ottomans upholstered with lime and orange fabrics, and suspending a tabletop from the ceiling. Gen adds classic Hollywood-style glamour to the Alpha Omicron Pi sorority chapter room by painting white and silver stripes on the walls, adding black and silver throw pillows, building a large armoire, and commissioning her team to trace silhouettes of Paige and herself for wall art.

after

before

Fashion Report: Paige sports horn-rimmed glasses at the start of the show.

Win Some, Lose Some

Doug's team fights to keep the existing beer lights in the room, rejecting the custom lights Doug wants to make. Doug eventually gives in.

Paint Fight!

When Doug points out that one of his team members missed a spot while painting, she paints his shirt. A full-fledged paint fight ensues.

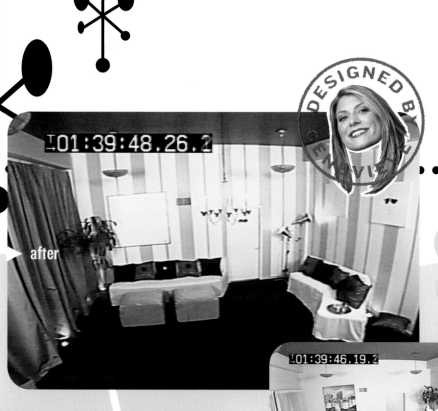
after

Shrewd Shopper
Gen calls around to buy a large carpet remnant for her room. When someone quotes her $500, she aggressively bargains down to $275.

before

Quotable Quote
Gen refers to the existing artwork in the room as something "straight out of the lobby at the women's clinic."

"Sexy, sexy, sexy!
—Gen's vision for a new couch"

Got a Match?
Gen, her homeowners, and Paige make a bonfire at the end of Day 1 to burn the existing draperies.

Bombs Away!
Doug is amazed by how filthy his assigned room is. When it's time to clear the room, Doug starts pitching everything out the third-story window—including the sofa. Later he has his team put on biohazard gear to sweep and clean the room before they start redecorating.

Gen's homeowners trace Paige and Gen's silhouettes to create stylized artwork.

Budget Buster

Both Gen and Doug end up going over budget. It's the first time both designers go over budget in an episode.

S2

E31

Oakland, CA: Webster Street

  ○ ⑦ ♥ | **Cast:** Paige, Genevieve, Hildi, Amy Wynn **Genevieve's Room:** ☺ ☺ ☹ | **Hildi's Room:** ☺ ☺ ☹

The Rooms

Hildi covers the walls of a living room with straw. She also installs a wall of bookshelves, covers the fireplace with copper mesh and glass rods, and screens the windows with wooden louvered blinds. Gen brightens a kitchen by painting the cabinets yellow and the walls cobalt blue, building a tile-top island and kids' table, personalizing dishware with family art and photos, and designing a backlit display shelf for a glass bottle collection.

after

The Last Straw

Hildi's wall treatment turns out to be high-maintenance. She and her homeowners spend much time brushing off straw that didn't adhere and hand-trimming long pieces.

before

DESIGNED BY HILDI

Reveal-ing Moment

The living room homeowners seem to like the design but are unsure about having straw on the walls with two young children in the household. When they demonstrate how the kids will pick at the straw, Paige eats two small pieces of straw.

Budget Buster

Hildi winds up over budget.

Demolition

Hildi and Amy Wynn demolish the existing mantel and bookshelves to install—surprise!—a different mantel and bookshelves.

after ⊤01:39:42.15

⊤01:39:40.00
before

Fashion Report: Gen has her hair wrapped in numerous tight little buns.

⊤01:21:54.2

Quotable Quotes

Hildi is truly amazed when one of her homeowners explains that the kids who will live in the home may tear straw off the walls and eat it. Hildi questions the homeowner's concern by asking, "Do they eat lint off of the sofa?" The homeowner tells her the children do. Hildi then asks, "Do they walk around outside and eat grass?" The homeowner tells her they do indeed.

Tearjerker: The kitchen homeowners love their room and cry happy tears.

⊤01:10:35.05

Color Crisis

Hildi tries to tint joint compound a reddish terra-cotta to use on the ceiling. It turns out pink. She uses it anyway.

S2 E32 California: Peralta Street

? ♥ | **Cast:** Paige, Doug, Hildi, Amy Wynn | Doug's Room: ☺ ☺ ☹ | Hildi's Room: ☺ ☺ ☹

The Rooms

Hildi divides a living room into quadrants by painting two opposite corners of the room and ceiling silver and painting the remaining corners and ceiling space violet. She covers the fireplace surround in a mosaic of clear glass, builds four aluminum chairs, and makes an ottoman upholstered in silk. Doug thinks pink in a dining room. He paints the walls bubble gum pink, paints the ceiling chocolate brown, hangs a lamp upside down from the ceiling, upholsters new white dining chairs with lime green T-shirts, and tops new storage units with green gazing balls.

before

after

DESIGNED BY HILDI

Forget-Me-Not
Hildi photographed parts of her own body to make wall art.

Plan B
Hildi attempts to drill through four large stones so she can attach them as legs on her ottoman. That doesn't work, so she has to use an adhesive to connect them.

Notable: During her Designer Chat, Hildi claims her room is one of her favorite designs ever.

Musical Moments

In this tuneful episode, the four homeowners play together in their band as Doug and Hildi dance together at the start of the show. Later Doug attempts to rap, and Hildi jokingly plays guitar while assigning homework to her team. For the finale Doug's male homeowner sings a song to Amy Wynn to entice her to do the necessary drywall work in the room. She refuses.

The Name Game

Doug doesn't officially title his room on-camera, but during the Designer Chat Paige refers to it as Pink Paradise.

Designer Power

Doug throws all the homeowners' knickknacks into the trash at the start of the show. Doug then reveals his paint colors to his homeowners by splashing the paint on a wall à la Jackson Pollock.

before

after

Once More, with Feeling

Doug and Paige repaint the dining room a darker, less pastel pink after the homeowners had already painted it with Doug's original choice of bubble gum pink.

Designer Chat

in which the designers have an opportunity to speak freely about their completed designs, their experiences with the homeowners, and the ups and downs they faced throughout the room transformation. This is also the stage at which the designers—and the viewers—learn who stayed under the $1,000 budget and who didn't. Here are some Designer Chats that feature favorite fashion moments and unforgettable exchanges between host and designer.

When Does the Movie Start?

Doug and Paige share a snack during Designer Chat. (Portland, OR: Everett Street, Season 2, Episode 26)

Party Time

Vern is under budget ($998.51), and he offers to take Paige out with his leftover funds because they "work like dogs" during the room transformations. (Indiana: Fieldhurst Lane, Season 3, Episode 21)

A Tip?

Hildi's $36.29 over budget. She pays Paige $50 and tells her to keep the change. (Orlando, FL: Smith Street, Season 3, Episode 46)

Slipcover Silliness

Paige and Gen put Gen's chair covers with the homeowners' faces over their heads and role play their reaction upon seeing them in their new room. (Colorado: Berry Avenue, Season 2, Episode 17)

Creative Clothing
Kia wears what appears to be several layers of multicolor printed fabrics, while Paige dons an Air Force jumpsuit. (Scott Air Force Base: Ash Creek, Season 3, Episode 24)

Frankly Fashionable
Frank wears a straw hat and a brown vinyl vest. (Philadelphia, PA: Strathmore Road, Season 1, Episode 10)

Pocket Change ...
Laurie is over budget by 11 cents. She gives Paige the change during her Designer Chat. (Santa Clara, CA: Lafayette Street, Season 2, Episode 27)

A Lesson in Contrasts
Edward wears an ascot tie, while Paige wears a *Trading Spaces* baseball jersey. (South Carolina: Sherborne Drive, Season 3, Episode 56)

Thanks, Paige!
Frank's $105 over budget. He pays Paige a $100 bill, and she says that she'll spot him the extra $5. (Orlando, FL: Whisper Lake, Season 3, Episode 54)

S2 E33 Los Angeles, CA: Willoughby Avenue

Cast: Paige, Doug, Genevieve, Ty   Doug's Room: ☺ ☹   Genevieve's Room: ☺ ☹

The Rooms

Doug sees red in a living room: He stencils the walls and doors in red and white, using a rectangular graphic based on an existing pillow pattern. He paints the ceiling gray, lays a red shag rug, and builds a U-shape couch with red upholstery. Gen designs a swingin' living room with 1950s flair by painting the walls aqua, disguising stains on the wood floor by painting it black, transforming mod place mats into wall sconces, slipcovering a futon in white vinyl, and laying a bookcase on its side to create a new coffee table.

Too Many Projects, Too Little Ty

Ty has too many projects and calls an executive meeting with Paige, Doug, and Gen. Doug agrees to give up a ceiling installation project so Ty will have time to finish Gen's projects.

Off-Key

Doug and his team sing loudly to annoy Gen's team, which is working in the room directly above.

Fashion Report

Gen wears a tube sock on her arm during Designer Chat. Doug's leather pants make an appearance, and he looks like he's growing a goatee. Paige wears a black top with feathers around the neckline.

> **"Hi, America. I'm Paige Davis. Look at my cute little Sandy Duncan hair."**
>
> **—Doug's male homeowner impersonating Paige**

after

DESIGNED BY GENEVIEVE

before

Back Atcha

Gen's team throws an old TV down the stairs to get back at Doug's team for singing so loudly. Paige and Doug convince Doug's homeowners that the noise was caused by their big-screen TV being accidentally dropped down the stairs. When the homeowners rush out to see the damage and realize it was a joke, one of them says, "Yea! Fun on The Learning Channel! Fun for everyone!"

Gen's Design Advice

"I think it's important whenever you do something that's remotely hip ... that you are able to update. Otherwise you're stuck in something that becomes very passé."

Reveal-ing Moment

Both male homeowners swear during The Reveals and have to be bleeped. All homeowners cry tears of joy when they come together at the end of the episode.

Flaming Success

Gen lights a cigar with a blowtorch when her room comes together and her team members announce they're done.

S2
E34

Los Angeles, CA: Springdale Drive

💣 $ | **Cast:** Paige, Laurie, Vern, Ty — Laurie's Room: ☺ 😐 ☹ | Vern's Room: ☺ 😐 ☹

The Rooms

Vern brightens a dining room by painting the walls yellow, hanging bronze draperies, installing a wall-length buffet with built-in storage, and designing a multiarmed halogen chandelier with gold vellum shades and a hanging candleholder. Laurie enlivens a basement den by painting the walls yellow, slipcovering the existing furniture with natural cotton duck fabric, sewing an aqua Roman shade, installing several yellow and aqua shadow box shelves, designing a folding screen to mask exercise equipment, and painting squares and rectangles in various shades of aqua to create custom wall art.

Demolition
Vern destroys a wall-length, built-in shelf with a rubber mallet.

Paint Problems

Vern's homeowners write positive thoughts on the walls in pencil, with the intent of painting over them as they work on the room. The writing shows through the paint, and they have to go back and clean off what they wrote before they finish painting the room.

Budget Buster: Laurie's basement design goes over budget.

Heavy Artillery

Ty isn't able to find studs in the wall to hang Laurie's shelves because there's a concrete or brick wall behind the Sheetrock. He has to use a special tool to drill and then use large bolts to hang the shadow box shelves.

S2 E38

Houston, TX: Sawdust Street

✳ ? $ ♥ | **Cast:** Paige, Doug, Laurie, Amy Wynn | **Doug's Room:** ☺ ☺ ☹ | **Laurie's Room:** ☺ ☺ ☹

The Rooms

Laurie refines a living room by painting the walls margarine yellow, building a wall-length bookshelf, hanging bamboo blinds and yellow drapery panels, and adding two spicy orange chairs. Doug goes "Zen/Goth" in a living room by painting the walls blood red, building an L-shape couch, hanging a large wrought-iron light fixture, adding a black faux fur rug, and enlarging a photo of the female homeowner in lingerie and knee-high boots to hang over the fireplace.

Budget Buster
Doug is nearly $50 over budget; he pays Paige in cash during his Designer Chat.

Notable: Laurie announces that she is pregnant.

Resourceful
Doug uses a long foam floatation device (pool noodle) to create bolster pillows for the couch. There's a sequence of scenes showing him taking it from kids in the pool area, who chase after him, yelling, "Give me back my noodle!"

Stirring Moment
Doug's homeowners are supposed to paint the fireplace black for their homework. They don't do the assignment, because when they opened their paint can, they thought the paint looked blue. Doug demonstrates that paint needs to be stirred, after which it looks black.

Panty Raid!
Doug finds a revealing photo to hang over the fireplace by digging through the female homeowner's drawers. She's shocked to see it during The Reveal.

Designer Favorite
The color palette and warmth of Laurie's room make it her favorite (that she's designed as a member of the *Trading Spaces* cast). She also believes this is one of the rooms that best reflects her personal style.

It's Outta Here: Both Doug and Laurie chuck the existing ceiling fans.

S2

E39

Houston, TX: Appalachian Trail

💣 ✳ $ | **Cast:** Paige, Doug, Laurie, Amy Wynn | **Doug's Room:** ☺ ☻ ☹ | **Laurie's Room:** ☺ ☻ ☹

after

The Rooms

Laurie adds style to an office/playroom by painting the walls terra-cotta, building a large shelving and desk unit with plumbing conduit, painting the existing coffee table and armoire in cream and black, adding new seating, and creating the illusion of symmetry with cream draperies on an off-center window. Doug goes for a soft look in a bedroom by painting the walls pale blue, upholstering a tall headboard in blue chenille, sewing new blue and white bed linens, and installing custom light fixtures.

DESIGNED BY LAURIE

before

Budget Buster
Laurie's multifunctional room isn't within the $1,000 limit; she's over budget.

Name Game: Doug titles his room A Pretty Room *by Doug*.

after

before

DESIGNED BY DOUG

Demolition
Amy Wynn and Doug's female homeowner take apart an existing bookshelf to reconfigure it.

Cheer Up!
Doug's female homeowner is a cheerleading coach. Her squad appears in the driveway and does a cheer for Doug: "Fix that space. You're an ace. Go, Doug, Go. You're a pro." Perhaps inspired by the cheerleading, Doug does a cartwheel later in the show.

Going, Going, Gone
Both Laurie and Doug remove the existing ceiling fans.

S2
E40

Plano, TX: Bent Horn Court

Cast: Paige, Genevieve, Vern, Ty

Genevieve's Room: ☺ ☺ ☹ | Vern's Room: ☺ ☺ ☹

The Rooms

Gen gets in touch with her inner child as she designs a playroom, painting multicolor polka dots on the walls, cutting movable circles of green outdoor carpeting for the floors, building a large castle-shape puppet theater, hanging fabric-covered tire swings, and designing four upholstered squares on wheels with storage space inside. Vern gets in touch with his rustic side in a living room by laying natural-color adhesive carpet tiles, painting an existing armoire and other furniture pieces black, and building a combination ottoman/coffee table/bench unit.

No Time for Paint
Ty makes Gen's wheeled squares at the last minute, and she doesn't have time to paint them. The tops are upholstered, but the sides are bare fiberboard during The Reveal.

Go, Girl
Gen sends Paige on a mission around the house to find objects with different textures that Gen can frame and hang as kid-friendly art.

Lucky Duck
Vern lucks out by finding a leather sofa and armchair in the house that work well in his design. He doesn't have to sew any slipcovers and uses the fabric for more pillows instead.

Fashion Report
Paige, Gen, and Ty all wear cowboy hats at the start of the show. Gen sports socks on her wrists again (Remember Los Angeles: Willoughby Avenue (Season 2, Episode 33?).

Tearjerker: The female living room homeowner cries tears of joy.

Plano, TX: Shady Valley Road

S2
E41

Cast: Paige, Doug, Hildi, Ty

Doug's Room: ☺ ☺ ☹ | **Hildi's Room:** ☺ ☺ ☹

The Rooms

Hildi creates a two-tone bedroom by painting the walls bright white, installing 12-inch-tall orange baseboards, building a new head- and footboard that match the pitch of the cathedral ceiling and covering them with white slipcovers, and upholstering a chair with white faux fur. Doug adds sophisticated style to a playroom by painting the wall moss green (Moss Madness), installing beams on the ceiling in a barnlike formation, building a basket-weave armoire, revamping a futon into a daybed, and hanging bifold doors on a toy closet.

after
before
DESIGNED BY HILDI

Paige and Ty bring Hildi a carpet remnant owned by her homeowners (left). Hildi tries to convince her female homeowner to allow her to dye the carpet (right).

Stress Alert

Hildi plans to dye the carpet in her room orange, but her female homeowner is adamantly opposed to the idea. They have several discussions about dyeing the carpet, with the homeowner becoming increasingly forceful in her opposition. At one point Hildi asks rhetorically why she's been asked to design the room if she's not going to be allowed to follow through on her vision. Then she notes, "Everyone in America knows I can dye that carpet if I want to." Hildi gives up at the end of Day 1, and the carpet stays white. (She problem-solves by sprinkling orange flower petals across the carpet for The Reveal.)

Old MacHildi Had a Farm
Hildi bottle feeds a baby goat during the B-Roll footage.

132

after

DESIGNED BY DOUG

before

Gifted

The two female homeowners are budding interior designers and have a business making draperies, table runners, and lamps. They present Paige with a small lamp during the Key Swap.

Notable

Doug and his female homeowner go fabric shopping with the PaigeCam at the end of Day 1.

S2

E42

Texas: Sutton Court

$ | **Cast:** Paige, Frank, Laurie, Ty   Frank's Room: ☺ ☺ ☹ | Laurie's Room: ☺ ☺ ☹

The Rooms

Laurie designs a kitchen, using the homeowners' china for inspiration. She paints the walls taupe with white trim, builds large wooden shadow boxes to display china pieces, hangs new light fixtures, and uses taupe fabric for the window treatments and chair cushions. Frank works with a Southwestern theme in a living room, adding chamois-cloth accents to the existing furniture, building a footstool out of a saddle, hanging several custom-made art pieces, designing a Mission-style armoire, and making potted "cacti" out of vegetables.

after

before

DESIGNED BY LAURIE

Budget Buster
Despite returning two rugs, Laurie winds up over budget.

Dapper Dog
Laurie's female homeowner features her dog in the introduction shots. She often dresses the dog in themed outfits, and it appears as a dragon and a cowboy during the show.

Subtle Change
Laurie's paint choices are close to the original colors in the room. The dining area is already the same shade of taupe as her main paint color, and the kitchen trim is already the same shade of white. Regardless, she sticks with her choices.

after

DESIGNED BY FRANK

before

Notable
Frank is hoarse throughout the episode and tells Paige, "I sound bad, but I am so perky."

Money Woes
Laurie and her homeowner are laying two rugs when Paige comes in to say that Laurie is already significantly over budget. Laurie doesn't believe it until Paige tells her that the wood cost twice as much as expected. Laurie sadly agrees to return the rugs to the store.

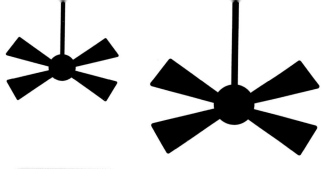

TCR 01:38.52.27

after

Reveal-ing Moments

Both sets of homeowners love their rooms, but the male living room homeowner swears twice upon opening his eyes and finding that the ceiling fan is gone. He vows to hang it up by the next morning.

TCR 01:38.50.15

before

Scrub-a-Dub-Dub

The upholstery on the existing off-white couch is soiled. Laurie is concerned because she had been told that the couch was in good condition, and she planned her whole design around it. She and her homeowners spend hours scrubbing the couch with heavy-duty cleaner and brushes.

Quotable Quote

In order to convince her homeowners that she must remove the existing ceiling fan, Laurie states, "I cannot in good faith do this room and not do this."

TCR 01:23.35.15

DESIGNED BY LAURIE

Season 3

The gang's all here! Kia, Edward, and Carter join the *Trading Spaces* team, and there are even a guest carpenter and plenty of celebrities to join the party.

8 Designers

$118,000 Total Budget

Celebrities

Air Force Base

The First Bathroom Makeover

59 Episodes

1 Host

236 Homeowners

4 Carpenters

Live Reveal

International Exchange

118 Room Transformations

S3
E1

Maine: George Road

Cast: Paige, Doug, Genevieve, Ty | Doug's Room: ☺ ☹ ☹ | Genevieve's Room: ☺ ☹ ☹

The Rooms

Doug adds warmth to a kitchen by painting the walls umber, painting the woodwork white, installing a butcher-block countertop, building a large pantry unit with bifold doors, and sewing a large tablecloth. Gen updates a dark kitchen by painting the walls bright green, installing a black and white tile countertop, building a butcher-block island, hanging wood laminate wall paneling, and installing a 1930s-style light fixture.

DESIGNED BY DOUG

after

before

Quotable Quotes

Doug's female homeowner tells her husband that Doug is "easy on the eyes." She goes on to say, "He hasn't been a real jerk yet."

Ty, Doug, and Paige installing a countertop (left). Gen grouting her new countertop (right).

Demolition
Doug, Ty, and Doug's homeowners remove the existing countertop before installing the new one.

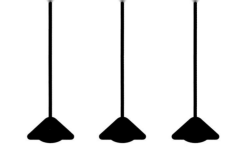

Budget Boasting

When Gen learns her budget is at $776.52, she looks into the camera and says, "Beat that, Doug!"

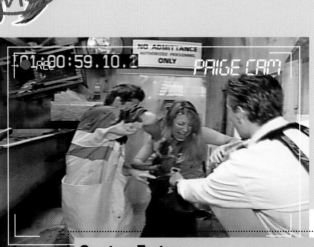

after

before

DESIGNED BY GENEVIEVE

Homeowner Woes

Gen's male homeowner says that he's worried about what's happening in his own house because he watched the episode featuring Doug's Pullman car bedroom (Maryland: Fairway Court, Season 2, Episode 13) the night before. He says, "Doug's scary."

Girl Power

When Gen's male homeowner gets a bit excited about working with a pretty young woman, Gen takes control of the situation, telling him, "If I can handle power tools, I can handle you."

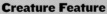

Creature Feature

Ty and Doug attempt to put live lobsters in Gen's hip waders during B-Roll footage.

S3
E2

Portland, OR: Rosemont Avenue

✳ | **Cast:** Paige, Laurie, Vern, Ty | Laurie's Room: ☺ ☺ ☹ | Vern's Room: ☺ ☺ ☹

The Rooms ●●●●●●

after

before

Laurie goes nautical in a living room by painting the walls deep aqua blue, painting the fireplace white, putting a cream-tone colorwash on wooden chairs and upholstering them with zebra-print fabric, and installing a vintage mercury glass chandelier. Vern brightens a living room by painting the walls yellow, hanging black and yellow Roman shades, installing French doors, covering the ceiling with white steel squares, hanging a ceiling fan, using black slipcovers for the existing furniture, and adding silver fold-up trays to serve as side tables and a coffee table.

Design Insight

Laurie says this is the first time that her paint color choice on *Trading Spaces* was not inspired by fabric. (Her inspiration in this case was the name of the paint color, which refers to the bay where the episode was filmed.)

Fan Ban: Laurie removes the existing ceiling fan.

Keyboard Crisis

Laurie struggles with the placement of a piano in her room. The home belongs to musicians who enjoy playing in their living room, but the floor joists aren't strong enough to hold the piano where Laurie wants to put it. She decides to leave the area empty and moves the piano to another room.

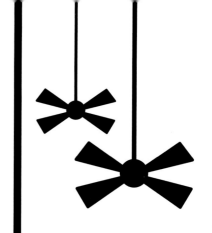

Making History
Vern actually installs an all-white ceiling fan in his room! He points out that it's a *Trading Spaces* first.

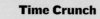

DESIGNED BY VERN

Time Crunch
Vern falls behind in his room because he and Ty have difficulties installing the French doors.

145

Maine: Joseph Drive

S3
E3

Cast: Paige, Frank, Laurie, Ty | Frank's Room: ☺ ☺ ☹ | Laurie's Room: ☺ ☺ ☹

The Rooms

Laurie enlivens a bedroom by painting the walls soft yellow, building an Asian-style shelving unit, designing a new headboard, sewing gray and white toile bedding, and adding an unusual floral light fixture. Frank shows another side of his design style in a bachelor's bedroom. He paints the walls and ceiling dark blue-green, hangs simple white draperies, sews a large plastic envelope to hold a pencil drawing of a leaf on the wall, builds a table that houses three wooden bins, and jazzes up a rocking chair with pet collars.

Notable: This is Laurie's last show before having her baby.

after

before

Stress Alert

Although painting the headboard was one of the homework tasks Laurie assigned, her homeowners are only starting to prime the piece on the morning of Day 2. Laurie wanted to do a faux finish but can't because the paint won't be dry in time. Frustrated, Laurie tells Paige, "I'm just so confused."

Fan Ban

Laurie removes the existing ceiling fan. She swaps it for an ornate gold light fixture that inspired the room's color palette.

Buckled In for Safety?

Frank straps pet collars on an existing rocking chair, explaining coyly that they can function as arm and leg restraints for visitors to the bachelor pad.

`01:43:27.20`

`01:39:40.27`

after

Huh?

Frank has his homeowners make art pieces with tar paper. He tells the homeowners he wants them to paint "a cave painting of a person who is very geometrically neat."

`01:39:39.11`

before

`:45.29`

Laugh Riot

Frank and one of his homeowners make custom candleholders with metal pipe nipples and flanges. The homeowner becomes giggly at the mention of "nipples," and she and Frank can't stop laughing throughout the project.

S3
E4

Long Island, NY: Steuben Boulevard

$ ◊ | **Cast:** Paige, Edward, Frank, Ty   Edward's Room: ☺ ☺ ☹ | Frank's Room: ☺ ☺ ☹

The Rooms

DESIGNED BY EDWARD

Edward jazzes up a bedroom by painting the walls light mocha, hanging wall sconces, building an Art Deco armoire, painting Deco patterns on the closet doors, installing lights around the bottom edge of the bed frame, hanging a canopy, and painting a faux-malachite finish on the furniture tops and wall sconces. Frank gets woodsy in a dining room, painting the walls deep orange, installing pine doors between the dining room and kitchen, creating a coffee table out of a large flowerpot, painting white birch trees all around the room, and making a large pig-topped weather vane to sit above the fireplace.

after

before †

Welcome!
This episode is Edward's *Trading Spaces* debut.

Tearjerker: The female dining room homeowner cries tears of joy.

DESIGNED BY FRANK

after

before

Dimension Discussion
Ty and Edward talk extensively about the armoire for Edward's room, but they can't agree on the dimensions. The finished piece ends up being too tall for the room, and Edward cuts off the feet to make it fit.

A Compliment?
Ty finishes installing the bed light, turns it on, and tells Edward, "It looks like Vegas!"

Shopping Savvy
Frank describes the bargain-hunting skills he used to purchase a rug at a home store: "I pitched such a wall-eyed fit about [the store] not having one wrapped in plastic that they gave me a 10 percent discount."

Budget Buster
Frank is slightly over budget. During his Designer Chat, he pays Paige the 79 cents he's over.

Long Island, NY: Split Rock Road

? | **Cast:** Paige, Genevieve, Vern, Amy Wynn | **Genevieve's Room:** ☺ ☺ ☹ | **Vern's Room:** ☺ ☺ ☹

after

before

The
Rooms

Gen brightens a dark kitchen by painting the walls white, the trim celadon green, the window shutters pale blue, and the cabinets yellow. Gen also polishes the existing copper stove hood, hangs white wooden slats on one wall, builds a butcher-block table, skirts the dining chairs in white fabric, and coats a new light fixture with copper spray paint. Vern adds a soft touch to a kitchen by painting the walls and cabinet door insets green, painting parts of the cabinet doors white, stenciling white fleurs-de-lis on the cabinet doors, building a new laminate countertop, laying a two-tone parquet floor, using green toile fabrics on Roman shades and table linens, adding touches of green gingham to the tablecloth, and adding several table lamps with green shades to the countertop.

Candleholder Crisis

Wanting to make candleholders out of rocks, Gen tries to drill into a rock with a carbide bit that she was assured could handle the job. (Didn't she remember the California: Peralta Street episode (Season 2, Episode 32) in which Hildi had similar problems?) After several attempts, Gen looks into the camera and says, "I suggest buying candleholders at the local hardware store."

Notable: Gen's inspiration for her design is a necklace that the female homeowner often wears.

after

Dance Break

Gen dances to shake a can of spray paint.

Hey, Isn't She ...

One of Vern's homeowners is the woman featured in a commercial that airs throughout Season 3.

before

Time Crunch

Before laying the parquet floor, Vern has to remove the existing linoleum floor. It has been glued down, and he spends most of Day 1 using a heat gun to loosen the adhesive.

S3
E6

New York: Whitlock Road

Cast: Paige, Doug, Genevieve, Amy Wynn | Doug's Room: ☺ ☺ ☹ | Genevieve's Room: ☺ ☺ ☹

The Rooms

Gen designs a bedroom with an espresso color scheme: She paints the walls café au lait, uses darker java on the ceiling beams, and paints sections of the ceiling cream. She also sews orange asterisks on a white bedspread, builds a combination headboard/desk, and exposes original wood flooring. Doug updates a bedroom by painting squares on the wall in multiple shades of sage, building a mantel-like headboard, designing S-shape side tables, sewing stripes of yarn on a white bedspread, and framing strips of wood veneer for bedside art.

after

DESIGNED BY GENEVIE

before

Budget Boasting

Gen's total costs amount to $763 and some change—the lowest budget quoted on camera thus far in the series.

Full of Hot Air

Gen and Amy Wynn shoot an air compressor hose into their mouths, blowing out their cheeks.

Stress Alert

Gen's male homeowner opposes every decision. Gen points out that they wouldn't have to argue about every choice if he would let the designer decide. The homeowners eventually wear her down, and she tells them to fight between themselves and pick a ceiling color; she'll do whatever they want. Later, when her male homeowner is complaining about her fabric choices, Gen mouths to the camera that after two days she'll be out of there and won't have to listen to him.

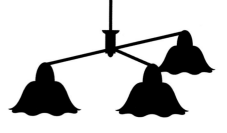

TCR 01:39.23:05

after

before

TCR 01:39.17:29

DESIGNED BY DOUG

Stress Alert 2

Doug's homeowners disagree with the bed placement, but he tells them that they don't get a choice. They put the bed where he wants it.

Stress Alert 3

Amy Wynn decides to change Doug's side table design due to structural concerns. When he finds out about it after the fact, he points out that he would like to be consulted before she makes any design decisions on his pieces in the future. She agrees and apologizes.

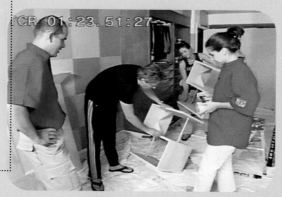

TCR 01:23.51:27

Fashion Report

Paige wears a tank top with removable hook-and-loop tape lettering. She customizes the shirt to feature phrases that relate to each scene of the show: Key Swap, Blue Team, Red Team, Gen, and Doug.

The Name Game: Doug titles his room Don't Box Me In.

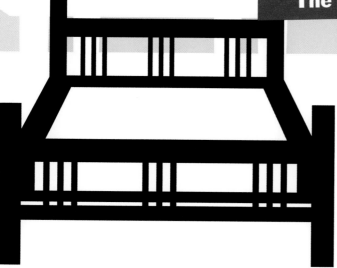

Faux Arrest

During the end credit shots, Paige is handcuffed by a local police officer and is escorted to a waiting police car.

S3

E7

New York: Half Hollow Turn

$ | **Cast:** Paige, Frank, Kia, Amy Wynn   Frank's Room: ☺ ☺ ☹ | Kia's Room: ☺ ☺ ☹

The Rooms

Frank updates a living room by painting the walls bamboo yellow, adding black accents on the walls and the furniture, using concrete stepping-stones to create side tables, converting a garden bench into a coffee table, and hanging a custom sculpture made from electrical and plumbing components. Kia gets funky in a basement rec room by painting the walls purple and light green, building a wall-length bench with purple velvet upholstery, hanging a swirly purple wallpaper border, installing halogen lights on a running cable, and creating green draperies.

Welcome: This episode is Kia's *Trading Spaces* debut.

Quotable Quotes

Frank describes his design idea as "transitional, cautious, contemporary." After finding a paint tray that hasn't been cleaned out, he tells his female homeowner, "As a nurse you should know … never leave a sponge in anything."

Budget Crisis

Paige uses too much spray paint on Frank's concrete stepping-stone project, but Frank doesn't have the money to buy more paint. Paige goes to Amy Wynn to figure out whether they can return enough of Frank's wood to buy the paint. They can and do.

after

before

Drapery Dilemma
One of Kia's homeowners fights Kia's decision to hang vertical blinds. Kia returns on Day 2 with fabric to create draperies instead.

Yum!
After the final Reveal, one of the homeowners presents a cake to Paige with the entire *Trading Spaces* cast airbrushed on the frosting.

Kia installing her first wallpaper border as a *Trading Spaces* designer.

" I will skulk out of here like the creep that I am and leave you to this horrible work. "
—Frank after assigning homework

153

S3	
E8	

Philadelphia, PA: 22nd Street

Cast: Paige, Edward, Genevieve, Ty   Edward's Room: ☺ ☹ ☺   Genevieve's Room: ☺ ☹ ☺

The Rooms

Edward adds ethnic flair to a living room by painting the walls red, texturing the fireplace with black paint and tissue paper, hanging an existing rug on the wall, building a chaise lounge with finial feet, and installing an entertainment center made of shadow boxes. Gen heads to Cuba in a bedroom by covering the walls with textured white paint, adding a faux-wood grain finish to the doors, building a headboard enhanced with a blown-up image from a Cuban cigar box, designing lighted plastic bed tables, and creating picture frames out of cigar boxes.

DESIGNED BY EDWARD

Edward's Design Advice
"You always have to have a grounding force of black in the room."

DESIGNED BY GENEVIEVE

Notable

Gen's inspiration for her room is the country of Cuba—although she's never been.

" When you're working with a $1,000 budget, you've got to faux it up a bit. "
—Gen

154

S3	
E9	# Philadelphia, PA: Gettysburg Lane

Cast: Paige, Frank, Vern, Ty   Frank's Room: ☺ ☺ ☹ | Vern's Room: ☺ ☺ ☹

The Rooms

Frank updates a kitchen by painting the walls and cabinets several different colors, laying stone-look vinyl floor tiles, installing a new countertop, adding decorative elements to a half-wall to create a new serving bar, and mounting plates with wooden food cutouts across the soffit. Vern adds his version of cottage style to a living room by painting the walls yellow, installing white wainscoting, building a 12-foot-wide shelving and storage unit, framing large copies of old family photos, making a "quilt" of images to hang above the storage unit, and adding touches of denim fabric throughout the room.

Quotable Quote

Frank's male homeowner tries to get out of faux-finishing, suggesting that it's a job for a woman. Frank says, "All of a sudden I feel like I have to go out and buy a dress for the prom because I do this all the time."

Tearjerker: The living room homeowners cry happy tears.

Time Crunch

Vern gets an unexpected head start on his room because the homeowners removed the existing wallpaper before the *Trading Spaces* team rolled into town. (The homeowners were afraid the designer would paint over the wallpaper.)

Fashion Report: For the first time, Vern wears shorts during the show.

Pennsylvania: Gorski Lane

 Cast: Paige, Doug, Frank, Ty | **Doug's Room:** ☺ ☺ ☹ | **Frank's Room:** ☺ ☺ ☹

The Rooms

Frank adds a celestial touch in a bedroom by painting the ceiling deep plum and painting silver stars across it. He covers the walls with several shades of cream and green paint, adds small blocks of color to the paneled doors, builds a writing desk, hangs a small cabinet upside down on the wall, and makes several pieces of custom artwork. Doug brings some "jungle boogie" to a bedroom by painting zebra stripes across all four walls, painting the ceiling dark brown, suspending a bamboo grid from the ceiling, and covering the existing headboard with sticks and bamboo.

DESIGNED BY FRANK

Quotable Quote
When Frank unveils his purple paint, he says to his homeowners, "Prepare yourselves for the final squeal."

The Blame Game
While Ty is helping one of Frank's homeowners install a ceiling fan, Ty's drill falls from his ladder and lands on the fan, shattering the glass. Frank rushes into the room and is speechless. Ty and the homeowner try to blame each other as Ty goes to stand in the corner. Ty eventually buys a new ceiling fan, paying for it himself so that it doesn't come out of Frank's budget.

> **" This is gonna be the funnest room I've ever done. "**
> —Doug

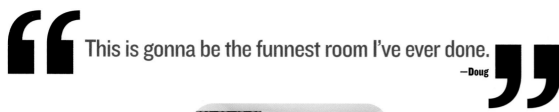

DESIGNED BY DOUG

01:39:42.02 *before*

1:39:45.21 *after*

Conflict

One of Doug's homeowners is very concerned about covering the walls with zebra stripes. As she tries to talk him out of doing it, Doug says, "There's no way you're gonna stop me, so don't even try."

01:20:52.12

Resourceful

Doug wants to include a table but doesn't have extra money in his budget to pay for lumber. Ty ends up digging through the trash for scrap timber to make it.

01:26:00.22

It's Raining Fruit ... Doug hangs real bananas on wire to accessorize his room.

01:00:52.01

Road Rage

During the opening Doug and Frank ride four-wheelers through a field. Frank wears a little blue helmet and pulls Ty behind him on a skateboard. Ty eventually falls off, and Frank stands next to him as Doug zooms by, indifferent to Ty's predicament. Frank shakes his head and mutters, "The compassion of a speed bump."

S3
E11

Long Island, NY: Dover Court

♥ | **Cast:** Paige, Edward, Vern, Amy Wynn | **Edward's Room:** ☺ 😐 ☹ | **Vern's Room:** ☺ 😐 ☹

The Rooms

after

Vern sets a boy's bedroom in motion by painting the walls various shades of blue, building a race car bed with working headlights, suspending a working train track and toy airplanes from the ceiling, hanging a motorcycle swing made from recycled tires, and hanging precut letters on the walls to spell out words like "woosh" and "zoom." Edward brings the outdoors into a bedroom by painting the walls moss green and antiquing a landscape print above the bed. He alters prefab side tables with filigree-like cuts, disguises the existing lamps with black spray paint and fabric slipcovers, hangs antique glass shutters over the windows, and builds a large entertainment center using the existing side tables and more glass shutters.

before

Mine!
Vern's male homeowner keeps saying "sweet," and Vern tries to claim the word is his.

Resourceful

Having heard that Vern is doing a "planes, trains, and automobiles" room, neighborhood kids want to give him pictures of all three to hang in the room. Vern likes the idea but points out that he doesn't have the money to pay them. The kids donate the pictures, which Vern then incorporates into the room.

Left Hand Blue
Vern and Paige work together to stencil dark blue airplanes onto the ceiling to look like shadows of the airplanes suspended below. Because they're working in such a small area, it's a bit like a Twister game as they reach across each other while holding the stencil in place.

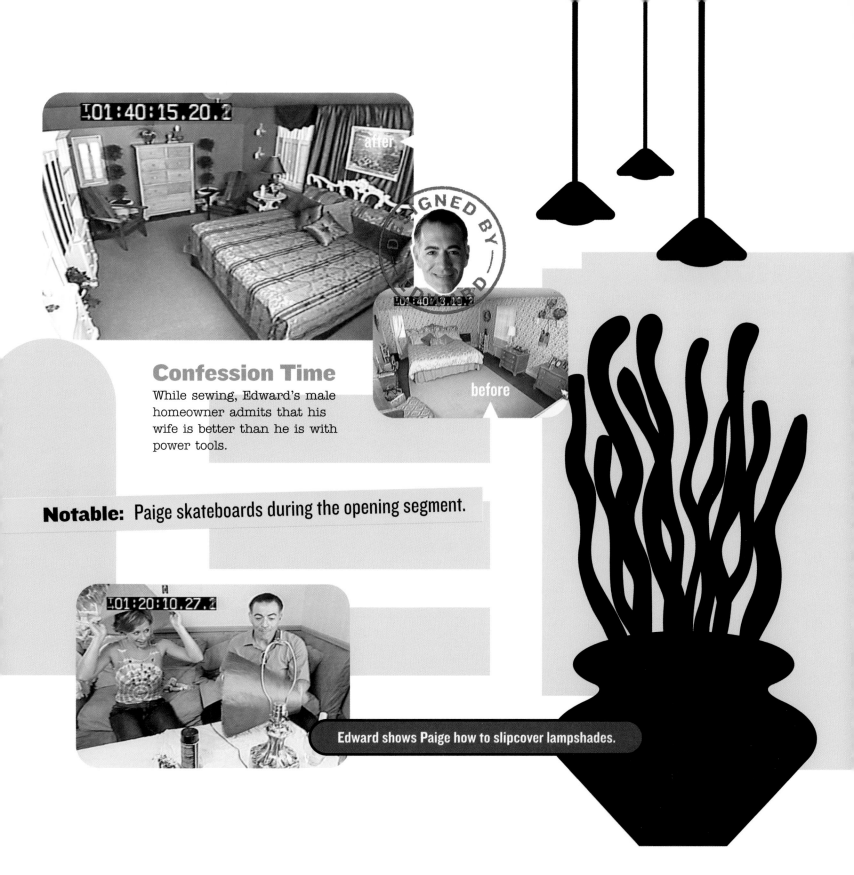

after

before

Confession Time

While sewing, Edward's male homeowner admits that his wife is better than he is with power tools.

Notable: Paige skateboards during the opening segment.

Edward shows Paige how to slipcover lampshades.

S3
E12

Pennsylvania: Victoria Drive

✳ ☺ ♥ | **Cast:** Paige, Doug, Kia, Amy Wynn | **Doug's Room:** ☺ ☹ ☹ | **Kia's Room:** ☺ ☹ ☹

The
Rooms

Doug creates a cabin feel in a living room by covering the walls in soft brown-tinted Venetian plaster, hanging red Roman shades, covering a ready-made coffee table with leather, staining the existing sofa and coffee tables a darker color, sewing cow-print throw pillows, building a large armoire covered with rough-cut poplar, and hanging leftover lumber on the walls in decorative stripes. Kia creates her version of an indoor garden in a guest bedroom by painting the walls yellow, hanging a flowery wallpaper border on the ceiling, creating a duvet from synthetic turf and silk flowers, building a headboard from a tree limb, hanging a chair swing from a cedar arbor, placing gravel under the swing, and building a picket-fence room divider.

after

before

No Thanks

When Doug's homeowners enter the room to meet him at the start of the show, Doug is barefoot, sitting on a window seat and enjoying a plate of brownies left for all of them by the other homeowners. Doug offers to share, but his team turns down the offer because Doug's feet are close to the plate. Doug then taps his foot across the top of the brownies and offers them again. He then sticks a piece of brownie between his toes and offers it to the homeowners. They don't take it.

Fan Ban: Doug removes the existing ceiling fan.

Stress Alert

Doug's homeowners are weary of working on the plaster walls and complain that waxing them isn't making a difference in how they look. Doug becomes short with them, saying that he takes a lot of pride in these finishes, and if they don't like it, they don't have to help.

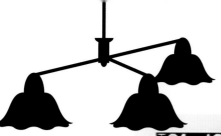

Oops!

The first cedar arbor that Amy Wynn builds for Kia's swing is too big to fit through the bedroom door, and Amy Wynn can't take it apart without ruining it. Kia doesn't have the budget to buy more cedar, so Amy Wynn pays for the extra wood to create a second arbor inside.

after

DESIGNED BY KIA

before

> I would not damage anything of quality. I only damage things that are crappy.
>
> —Doug

Fashion Report

Doug dons a cowboy hat in several scenes. In keeping with the theme of her room, Kia wears overalls and a straw hat.

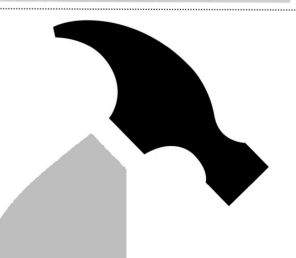

161

S3
E13

New Jersey: Manitoba Trail

Cast: Paige, Doug, Frank, Amy Wynn   **Doug's Room:** ☺ ☺ ☹ | **Frank's Room:** ☺ ☺ ☹

The Rooms

Frank goes all out in a country living/dining room by painting the walls light green, distressing the wood floors, painting a faux rug beneath the coffee table, applying several decorative paint colors and finishes to an antique cabinet, building custom lamps with large antique yarn spools, and creating three homemade country-girl dolls with pillow forms. Doug brightens a living room by painting everything—the walls, ceiling, ceiling beams, fireplace, and ceiling fans—bright white (White Whoa). He buys two new white sofas, hangs bright blue draperies, installs a new doorbell that blends into the white wall, sews many brightly colored throw pillows, makes a large framed mirror, and creates custom art pieces.

after

before

DESIGNED BY FRANK

Quotable Quote

Because one of his homeowners is experiencing soreness in her neck and shoulders from a recent accident, Frank tells her to go rest; he says he'll stay and do her homework. Frank then puts on her smock and impersonates her, saying, "I can't believe that little, fat, rotund twerp gave us all this homework after we worked all that time."

Foot Fetish

Doug goes barefoot while painting a white border on a natural rug and puts his bare feet near his female homeowner's head while she sews pillows.

after

before

DESIGNED BY DOUG

Reveal-ing Moment

The male country living/dining room homeowner is so happy about his room that he kisses Paige on the cheek.

Nazareth, PA: First Street

 | **Cast:** Paige, Doug, Vern, Amy Wynn | **Doug's Room:** ☺ ☹ ☺ | **Vern's Room:** ☺ ☹ ☺

The Rooms

Vern adds a touch of serenity to a living room by painting three walls taupe and one wall deep blue, adding a new mantel, sewing throw pillows with a wave-motif fabric, suspending mini symbiotic environments from the ceiling, building a coffee table with a center inset of sand and candles, and placing six fountains around the fireplace. Doug gives a kitchen an earthy feel by laying brown peel-and-stick vinyl flooring, painting the walls beige, installing new orange laminate countertops, painting the cabinets yellow with an orange glaze, adding crown molding to the cabinet tops, building a pie safe, and upholstering the dining chairs with red-orange fabric.

Earthy Inspiration

Vern's sand-and-sea design springs from the homeowners' love of the beach and the desert.

I See Paris ...

Vern's fire suit falls down as he's running during the opening segment, exposing a pair of jeans beneath.

DEMOLITION

Vern rips out the existing mantel.

Sorry, Small Sample

Doug's countertop turns out to have a wood grain. When he ordered it, he thought it was solid orange based on the sample chip he had. It was too late to do anything about it, though, because it arrived late on Day 2.

Notable

Amy Wynn and Doug have a food fight during the end credits.

163

S3 E15 New Jersey: Catania Court

✳ $ | **Cast:** Paige, Genevieve, Hildi, Amy Wynn | Genevieve's Room: ☺ 😐 ☹ | Hildi's Room: ☺ 😐 ☹

The Rooms

Hildi has the golden touch in a bedroom: She paints the walls pea green, sews bedding with fabrics she purchased in India, uses batik-print stamps to create gold accents on the ceiling and around the room, replaces the existing baseboards with taller ones, adds a gold wash to the existing furniture, builds a low-slung "opium couch," and hangs a vintage glass light fixture. Gen finds the silver lining in a dining room: She paints the walls orange-red, hangs silver crown molding, paints the trim and chair rail ivory, hangs ivory and silver draperies, paints a canvas floorcloth to lay under the table, and hangs a new light fixture that has small tree limbs attached to it.

after
before
DESIGNED BY HILDI

Fashion Report
Hildi's male homeowner starts the show wearing heels, noting that he's chosen "Hildi-approved footwear."

Fan Ban: Hildi removes the existing ceiling fan.

Budget Crisis
Hildi's walls are sucking up the paint, and there isn't enough to finish a first coat, so she has to buy more paint. When her homeowner asks if it's going to be OK, she says it won't because she doesn't have enough money to buy more paint. Somehow she resolves the problem, and she's under budget at the end of the show.

Wallpaper Woes

Gen accidentally cuts wallpaper strips too short to hang on the walls. She eventually says, "Only serious professionals need apply for this job!"

after
before
DESIGNED GENEVIEVE

We're Counting
For the second time in the series, Gen reveals her fabric choices by wearing them as a toga.

Ringing Inspiration
Gen gets her design idea from a piece of her own jewelry, a ring from Afghanistan.

S3
E16

Philadelphia, PA: East Avenue

? | **Cast:** Paige, Frank, Hildi, Amy Wynn | Frank's Room: ☺ ☺ ☹ | Hildi's Room: ☺ ☺ ☹

after

before

DESIGNED BY HILDI

The
Rooms

Hildi gets graphic in a living room by painting three walls yellow, covering one wall with a large Lichtenstein-inspired portrait of herself, adding a glass-shelf bar area, building all new tables and chairs, sewing cushions with mod pink and orange fabric, and re-covering a thrift store couch with red fabric. Frank brightens a living room by painting the walls deep purple, painting the ceiling bright red, designing a coffee table unit with four bases that move apart and become extra seating, and creating wall art with rain gutter materials and round wooden cutouts.

Stormy Weather

An overnight storm ruins Hildi's lumber, throwing all her projects into peril. (Hmmm, remember Hildi's spray-painted couch fiasco in Seattle: 56th Place (Season 2, Episode 23?)

Seeing Spots

Hildi's wall-size self-portrait takes her team nearly both days to paint with tiny little dots.

after

before

TCR 01:39.28.19

DESIGNED BY FRANK

Resourceful

After applying one coat of purple paint onto the wall, Frank realizes that the original burgundy paint is showing through in patches, creating an unexpected faux finish. He decides to keep it that way.

Quotable Quote

While hanging draperies, Frank dispenses his wisdom, saying, "A little fluffing is good."

S3

E17

Virginia: Gentle Heights Court

💧 💲 ♥ | **Cast:** Paige, Hildi, Kia, Ty | Hildi's Room: ☺ 😐 ☹ | Kia's Room: ☺ 😐 ☹

The Rooms

Hildi sets up camp in a boy's bedroom by painting the walls and ceiling midnight blue, hanging a moon-shape light fixture, placing glow-in-the-dark stars on the ceiling, hanging a solar system mobile, building a 13-foot-tall rock climbing wall, adding several pieces of fold-up camping furniture, placing the mattress in a room-size tent, using a blue sleeping bag as a duvet, and placing camping lanterns around the room. Kia adds sensuous details to a bedroom by painting the walls orange and the trim Grecian blue, hanging a red and gold wallpaper border, creating a Taj Mahal cutout to place around the existing entertainment center, installing two wooden columns from India, adding bedding made from sari fabrics, and suspending the bed from the ceiling with chains.

after

before

Notable

Paige doesn't swap the keys: She holds a dry-erase board and draws football plays on it, and the homeowners switch keys with each other.

Guy Stuff

Ty (wearing a bike helmet for safety) and Hildi's male homeowner try out the completed rock wall. They jokingly fall on top of each other on the floor.

Tearjerker: The boy's room mother cries happy tears.

Midnight Carpentry

Ty must work late into Day 1 to complete Kia's Indian column project. He uses the PaigeCam to record himself working (and lamenting the fact that he is working).

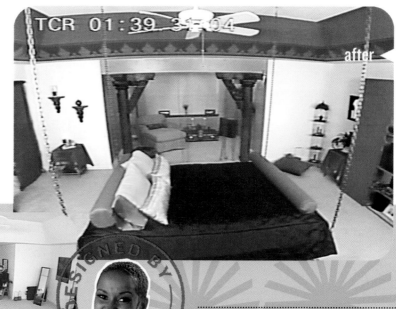

after

Budget Buster

Kia's wooden columns aren't tall enough to reach the ceiling; they have to be secured with an extra wooden header. Buying the additional wood puts her over budget.

before

Quotable Quote

When Kia asks Ty when he's going to hang the chains for her bed, he says, "Just as soon as you're through yanking mine."

Designer Favorites

This is an episode of favorites! Kia says her hanging bed design is one of her favorite projects; she sleeps in one herself! For Hildi, The Reveal for this room was memorable: "This show proved the joy of creating a fantasy for this little boy. The expression on his face was priceless; it brought tears to my eyes."

Kia checks on Ty while he's installing the bolts for the bed in the ceiling joists (left). Kia and her homeowners test the strength of the bolts Ty installed (right).

Reveal-ing Moments

Upon seeing the suspended bed in her newly decorated room, the female homeowner exclaims, "I wanna jump in there and get naked!"

Fashion Report: A shirtless Ty suns himself during the end credits.

Reveals

The Reveal! Anxious homeowners finally have an opportunity to see how their neighbors, with the help of a *Trading Spaces* designer, re-created their rooms. Will they love it? Dislike it? Will they laugh? Cry? Curse? Storm out of the room? Kiss the host? Here are some of the best-known reactions and best-loved Re-vealing moments.

I Swear!

The living room homeowners seem to like the design but are very unsure of having straw on the walls because they have two young children. Paige eats two small pieces of straw, demonstrating what the kids will likely do. The female homeowner eventually swears and has to be bleeped. (Oakland, CA: Webster Street, Season 2, Episode 31)

Here's the Dish ...

After seeing their black dining room, the male homeowner says, "I don't think it's that bad." His wife quickly replies, "I don't think it's that good." (Pennsylvania, PA: Bryant Court, Season 3, Episode 58)

Happy Days

When the two sets of homeowners come together in the end, the women start crying—and everyone's reaching quickly to hug each other, knocking Paige backward in the melee. (Miramar, FL: Avenue 164, Season 3, Episode 45)

They Love It!

Both sets of homeowners love their rooms, and the kitchen homeowners won't stop screeching. Paige eventually puts her fingers in her ears. (Texas: Sherwood Street, Season 2, Episode 37)

Everyone Knows Her Name ...

It's Pam. After seeing her slipcovered fireplace, she leaves the room in tears. (Seattle, WA: 137th Street, Season 2, Episode 21)

She's a Keeper

The male bedroom homeowner is so happy, he kisses Paige on both cheeks. His new wife is so grateful, she says she doesn't even care that he's kissing another woman. (Washington, D.C.: Quebec Place, Season 3, Episode 19)

Rueful Reveal

Sarah Rue's disappointed when she sees her redecorated office and describes the wall color as "a garbage can kind of gray." (Los Angeles, CA: Elm Street, Season 3, Episode 48)

Wine-Label Woes

The kitchen homeowners, who don't drink alcohol, aren't thrilled with the wine labels adhered to their walls. (Austin, TX: Wyoming Valley Drive, Season 3, Episode 30)

One Satisfied Customer!

The little girl who resides in the room loves the redesign. Her mother sees her daughter's new monkey desk and exclaims, "You have a bar!" (Scottsdale, AZ: Bell Road, Season 3, Episode 38)

Unhappy Days

The purple/gray living room homeowners strongly dislike their room. The husband says, "We've got the set of the *Dating Game* on our walls" and "Beetlejuice lives here." (Philadelphia, PA: Strathmore Road, Season 1, Episode 10)

Arlington, VA: First Road

💣 ✳ 👶❓♥ | **Cast:** Paige, Doug, Hildi, Ty | **Doug's Room:** ☺ ☹ ☹ | **Hildi's Room:** ☺ ☹ ☹

The Rooms

Hildi gift-wraps a bedroom by painting the walls "Tiffany box" aqua blue, adding a duvet and Roman shades in the same aqua blue, airbrushing white "ribbons" on the walls and fabrics, hanging white lamps with square shades above the headboard, building acrylic side tables that light up from inside, and adding bright silver accents. Doug warms up a bedroom by painting the walls and ceiling a deep gray-blue; hanging white Roman shades, brown silk curtains, and cornice boards; constructing a headboard from a large existing window frame; visually balancing the headboard with a new armoire that features white silk door insets; and creating custom artwork in brown and navy.

after

before

DESIGNED BY HILDI

Fan Ban
Both Hildi and Doug remove the existing ceiling fans.

Notable
Hildi's male homeowner leaves an apology note on the wall in black marker. It says, "Dude, they made me do it!"

Homework Headaches
For homework, Hildi has her team airbrush the "ribbons" on the walls. When she returns on Day 2, the project is complete but not quite the way she would have done it. Hildi tries to keep a positive attitude and says, "It's fine."

Demolition
Hildi removes the existing chair rail.

> **" "** I can't continue to educate people on what's good taste!
> —Doug

TCR 01:38.57.26

after

DESIGNED BY DOUG

TCR 01:38.54.19

before

The Mother of All Stress Alerts

Doug's homeowners disagree with every decision, including the removal of the ceiling fan, the chosen paint colors, painting the ceiling, staining the floor, and accessorizing the room. At one point, Doug tells them, "I've done 30-some *Trading Spaces* episodes. I know what ... I'm doing." Near the end of Day 1, Doug washes his hands of the room and uses the PaigeCam to record instructions for making draperies.

The Name Game

Doug titles his room Framed.

Reconciliation

While Doug is reclining in a lawn chair reading a newspaper, his homeowners come to say that they need him after all. By the end of Day 2, Doug's female homeowner admits that the design is growing on her. Doug says, "It's growing on her like a fungus, but it's growing."

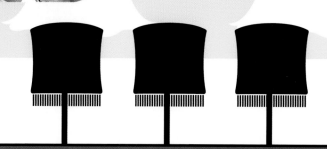

Notable: Doug drinks from a mug that reads, "Damn, I'm good."

S3	**Washington, D.C.:** Quebec Place
E19	

✳ | **Cast:** Paige, Genevieve, Vern, Ty   **Genevieve's Room:** ☺ ☺ ☹ | **Vern's Room:** ☺ ☺ ☹

The Rooms

Gen dishes up a serene living room inspired by her favorite Thai soup. She paints the walls a light bone color and gives the room lemongrass green accents, a newly constructed sofa, a wall-length valance with lemongrass curtains, and lotus flower light fixtures. Vern turns up the heat in a newlywed couple's bedroom by painting the fireplace and dressing room red, installing a floor-to-ceiling mirrored wall in the dressing area, hanging rows of crystals above the fireplace, sewing red silk Roman shades, and installing a large headboard with red silk insets.

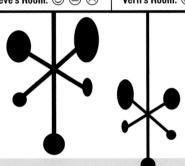

DESIGNED BY GENEVIEVE

before

L01:38:39.21

after

Fashion Report

High heels abound in this episode: Both female homeowners wear them during the Key Swap and The Reveal; Gen wears them when first meeting her homeowners. Comfort and practicality win out, and everyone quickly removes the shoes and works barefoot.

Cornice Board Confusion
When Ty attempts to install a wall-length cornice board he built for Gen's room, he discovers that he built it 1 foot too long. Much discussion ensues, and Ty eventually cuts 6 inches from each end.

Time Crunch

Gen asks her homeowners to create custom artwork inspired by artist M. C. Escher. They make several valiant attempts, but Gen eventually tells Paige, "No one has time for Escher today," and scraps their drawings for framed pieces of printed fabric for the room.

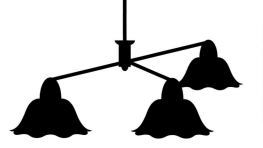

Head Games

Vern's headboard is so large and unwieldy that he has to have a police car stop traffic so that he and his homeowner can carry it across the street. After they get it inside, they find the piece is too large to go up a flight of stairs, and Ty has to cut a portion off the bottom to resolve the situation.

after

Resourceful

Vern initially planned to restore the hardwood floor in his room by cleaning it, but by the end of Day 2, he shows Paige the large red rug he has purchased to hide the floor, which is not shaping up as he had hoped.

Fan Ban: Vern removes an existing ceiling fan.

Well, Thanks

Gen tells Ty that the couch he built is her favorite piece of furniture he's created during the series. She also tells her homeowners that their stain job on the sofa frame is the best anyone has done on the show.

before

DESIGNED BY VERN

Notable

This episode is the first time Kia's and Edward's faces appear among the quick shots of the designers during the opening credits.

Reveal-ing Moments

The male homeowner on one of the teams is so happy that he kisses Paige on both cheeks. His wife likes the makeover so much, she says she doesn't even care that he's kissing another woman.

S3 E20

Indiana: River Valley Drive

Cast: Paige, Doug, Genevieve, Amy Wynn   Doug's Room: ☺ ☺ ☹ | Genevieve's Room: ☺ ☺ ☹

The Rooms

Gen tones down a brightly colored living room by painting the walls a sleek silver-gray; painting the existing furniture white; designing a new entertainment center made out of stacked white boxes with punched-aluminum door insets; and adding a few bold touches of color with green curtains, a new green room screen, and a fuchsia ottoman. Doug puts his foot down in his Back from Brazil living room, hanging a three-section painting of his own foot. He also stencils white flowers—inspired by sarongs— on the walls, slipcovers the existing furniture in white, highlights the fireplace mantel with a large vertical wooden extension, designs an acrylic light fixture, and sews throw pillows from tie-dyed sarongs.

after

before

Musical Moment
Gen plays guitar for Amy Wynn during the end credits, making up a song about kicking Amy Wynn's "butt" if she doesn't finish her carpentry projects.

after

Reveal-ing Moments
The silver living room homeowners exclaim, "We're not changing a thing!" The Brazil living room homeowners seem confused by the flower stenciling and ask, "What is that? An olive?"

Playing Footsie
Gen's female homeowner hates feet. Gen, who is barefoot, encourages her male homeowner to work barefoot too, and the two run their bare feet up and down the female homeowner's legs. Gen eventually convinces her female homeowner to go barefoot. She removes her shoes and socks, revealing carefully manicured feet and a silver toe ring.

This Little Piggy ...
Doug gets into the episode's foot-centric attitude by clipping and cleaning his toenails when his team enters the room to meet him for the first time. He continues to do so during Load Out (his homeowners do the work).

before

S3
E21

Indiana: Fieldhurst Lane

Cast: Paige, Doug, Vern, Amy Wynn

Doug's Room: ☺ ☺ ☹ | **Vern's Room:** ☺ ☺ ☹

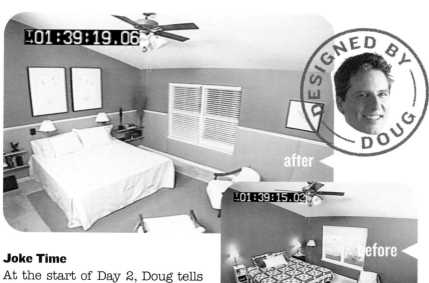

after

before

The Rooms

Doug gets back to his Midwestern roots in a bedroom by painting the walls orange, installing wainscoting upholstered with tan fabric, creating custom paintings of wheat and corn, embellishing simple white bedding with orange ribbon and yarn, and designing a large armoire. Vern sets a restful scene in a bedroom by painting the walls a light blue, attaching oak plywood squares to a wall, painting the existing furniture black, reupholstering a chaise lounge with dark blue velvet, hanging blue velvet draperies, wrapping the bed frame with white beaded garland, and installing new sconces and a ceiling fixture with white beaded shades.

DESIGNED BY DOUG

Joke Time
At the start of Day 2, Doug tells his homeowners that he doesn't like the bright orange walls and that they're going to have to repaint them light green. Paige tells Doug no, Doug insists, and they storm off arguing. Doug reenters with brushes and starts repainting over the orange paint himself. When the homeowners finally relent and pick up brushes, Doug laughs and says, "Gotcha!" His female homeowner gets the last laugh, though, slapping Doug's face with her green paint-covered brush.

Kiss-Off
When Paige says goodbye at the end of the show, all four homeowners blow a kiss toward the camera á la *The Dating Game*.

after

before

DESIGNED VERN

Notable
The blue team ends up with a blue bedroom, and the orange team ends up with an orange bedroom.

Fan Ban
Vern removes the existing ceiling fan.

Tearjerker
The orange bedroom's female homeowner starts crying nervous tears before she's even opened her eyes to see the room.

S3 E22 Indianapolis, IN: Halleck Way

✳ 👶 ⑦ $ ♥ | **Cast:** Paige, Edward, Kia, Amy Wynn | **Edward's Room:** ☺ ☺ ☹ | **Kia's Room:** ☺ ☺ ☹

The Rooms

Edward designs a soft yet masculine bedroom by painting the tray ceiling slate blue and white, painting the walls and existing furniture tan, hanging a customized light fixture with a hand-painted glass frame, draping white fabric across the length of one wall, hanging brown draperies made from lush fabrics, and slipcovering the head- and footboards. He also rearranges the furniture and creates neoclassic wall shelves. Kia creates an Egyptian theme in a bedroom by painting the walls Tut Wine and Pharaoh Gold, building pyramid-shape cornice boards, and hanging framed Egyptian prints and a handmade Eye of Horace. She also paints a personalized hieroglyphic message for the homeowners ("David loves Noel") on an existing room screen and installs a ceiling fan with palm leaves attached to the blades.

L01:37:41.06 after

L01:37:36.12 before

DESIGNED BY EDWARD

Vroom

Edward drives a race car with Kia as his passenger at the Indianapolis Motor Speedway during B-Roll footage. Amy Wynn waves the checkered flag.

Creative Craftiness
Edward creates his own drapery rods by covering cardboard tubes with fabric, gluing the ends inside the tube, covering plastic foam balls with fabric, and attaching them to the ends as finials.

Notable: During a bumper shot, Paige enters wrapped up in gauze like a mummy.

Quotable Quote
Toward the end of Day 2, Edward is falling behind and tells Paige that the room is "kind of coming together." Paige responds by saying, "Yeah, if you stress the words 'kind of.'"

DESIGNED BY

01:35:07.26

01:35:39.29

01:37:46.20

after

Pyramid Problems

Kia spends much of her budget on a pyramid-shape fountain that she designed herself. The fountain is the subject of many discussions, including questions about its construction, sealant, and pump mechanism. Although she is skeptical about the fountain functioning, Amy Wynn works on this while squatting in the homeowners' water-filled bathtub. Late on Day 2, Kia and her team meet with Amy Wynn—and an obviously leaky fountain. They decide to chuck the whole thing at the last minute.

01:37:44.10

before

Back to the Drawing Board

During the Designer Chat, Paige asks Kia if she'll ever try to make another pyramid fountain. Kia says that she may try to perfect her design, prompting Paige to ask, "So, homeowners beware?"

01:15:26.11

Stress Alert!
Early in Day 1, Kia's homeowners run out of paint during the first coat. Kia questions the homeowners' painting ability. Paige thinks it's Kia's paint calculations. Kia eventually gives the homeowners a painting lesson in an attempt to salvage what paint she has left, but she must buy another gallon.

S3
E23

Missouri: Sunburst Drive

✳ | **Cast:** Paige, Genevieve, Vern, Ty | **Genevieve's Room:** ☺ ☺ ☹ | **Vern's Room:** ☺ ☺ ☹

The Rooms

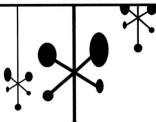

01:38:39.04.1 before

Gen draws inspiration for a bedroom from gauchos (Argentine cowboys). She paints the walls deep brown, creates faux crown molding by bringing the ceiling paint several inches down onto the walls, installs a woven leather-and-red-velvet headboard, and glues pictures of gauchos to the closet doors. She also builds an upholstered bench and pulls in furniture from other rooms that complements the room's color scheme. Vern adds a masculine edge to a girlie bedroom by painting the walls soft blue, painting the existing furniture and doors red, designing a wall-length desk and computer hutch, installing a headboard made of upholstered leather squares, and adding several wrought-iron light fixtures and Moroccan-inspired accents.

01:38:40.21 PLAY after

DESIGNED BY GENEVIEVE

Silly Gen!

Paige chastises Gen and her team for falling behind on Day 1, asking them what they've gotten done. Gen sheepishly replies, "We've laughed a lot."

More Gen

While working with her female homeowner to upholster a bench, Gen shows her how to use cardboard to keep a straight, professional-looking line when finishing off the edges. She then says jokingly under her breath, "Because that's all we are on this show— a bunch of professionals."

Headboard Headaches

Ty has multiple problems while installing Gen's leather headboard: He bumps heads—literally— with Gen's male homeowner, and after spending a lot of time attaching the headboard to the wall, he stands back and realizes the headboard is slightly off-center. They debate whether it's worth fixing. The problem is resolved off-camera.

> **"** Some days it goes quickly. Some days it just doesn't. **"**
> —Ty sums up *Trading Spaces*

DESIGNED BY VERN

after

Fashion Report

The cast members wear monogrammed bowling shirts and bowl during the B-Roll footage. Gen bowls barefoot.

Shake It!

Gen, Paige, and Gen's homeowners dance during a quick bumper shot. Vern dances on another.

Time Crunch

There isn't time to install all the doors on the computer hutch, so Vern leaves the remaining pieces for the homeowners to attach later.

before

"Do you like clean lines and straight things? Vern does.

—Gen to her female homeowner on what Vern may be doing next door"

Thrown Out

Vern removes an existing ceiling fan.

Watch For
There are several fun filming bloopers during the end credits.

S3 E24 Scott Air Force Base, MO: Ash Creek

💧 ❓ | **Cast:** Paige, Doug, Kia, Ty   **Doug's Room:** ☺ 😐 ☹ | **Kia's Room:** ☺ 😐 ☹

The Rooms

Doug travels down Route 66 in a child's bedroom by laying gray carpet, painting highway stripes and road signs on the walls, and installing a front and back end from two actual cars. (He adds a mattress in the back end of one car, and the front end of the other car serves as a toy chest.) Kia creates Military Chic in a living/dining room, using various shades of gray paint, new chair rails, a gray and white camouflage wallpaper border, pillows and cushions in the same camouflage color combination, a new storage bench, a faux fireplace, a red slipcover, red decorative accents, and draperies made from a gray parachute.

Family Ties

As Doug reveals his design idea to Ty, a semitrailer truck arrives, loaded with the two car halves. It then becomes a circus act, as seven people start filing out of the cab. Doug introduces them as his brothers, nephews, and friends—all of whom are there to help carry the car halves into the room.

Designer Favorites

Kia says the room Doug designed for this episode is one of her favorites created by a fellow castmate.

Car-nival

Getting the cars into the room is difficult and time-consuming. The front end doesn't fit down the hallway and has to be sawed in half and reassembled inside the room. Ty spends so much time on Doug's cars that he has to eliminate one of Kia's projects.

Take It Easy

During Load Out, Doug sits in a child's chair as his homeowners do all the work. They eventually carry the chair out of the room—with Doug in it.

after

before

Musical Chairs
Late on Day 2, Kia can't decide how she wants to lay out the furniture. After trying several different arrangements, Paige tells Kia to make up her mind because she's out of time.

DESIGNED BY KIA

Fashion Report
During Designer Chat, Kia wears an outfit that seems to consist of several layers of multicolor printed fabrics.

Drop In
Kia meets her homeowners after having supposedly parachuted onto the roof.

Shocking Confession
Kia admits to her female homeowner that she's "never used a slipcover before."

Ten Hut!
General Handy, a four-star general, visits Doug's room as it's in progress and asks the question on everyone's mind: "A car in a bedroom?"

Tearjerker: The female living room homeowner is disappointed with her room and cries.

S3
E25

Missouri: Sweetbriar Lane

Cast: Paige, Edward, Frank, Ty

Edward's Room: ☺ ☺ ☹ | Frank's Room: ☺ ☺ ☹

DESIGNED BY EDWARD

The Rooms

Edward designs a sleek bedroom by painting the walls shades of gray, white, and China blue; adding extra closet and storage space; and designing a mirrored entertainment armoire to conceal the TV. He also hangs a light fixture wrapped in pearls; adds gray, purple, blue, and green fabrics; and creates a sculpture from curled metal. Frank creates an eclectic bedroom, painting the walls orange and installing large eyes made of copper tubing above the bed. An upholstered lip headboard completes the face, and a new platform bed stands beneath it. Frank paints the fireplace purple and creates an artistic theme by attaching a giant pencil on one wall and painting female figures near it to look as though they'd been sketched.

after

before

Heavy Metal

Gushing about his metal sculpture during Designer Chat, Edward tells Paige that he wants to make more pieces like it because he enjoyed the sparks flying when he sawed into the metal.

The Great Paige-kin

During the beginning shots of the homeowners, one set is carving a *Trading Spaces* jack-o'-lantern complete with Paige's face.

Quotable Quote

Frank tells Paige that he used her lips as inspiration for his headboard. She's impressed that he noticed her lips, and he replies, "I may be old, but I'm not dead."

TCR 01:39.10:03

after

Ouch?

During the Carpenter Consult, Frank jokingly knocks Ty to the ground. Ty milks the experience by wearing a neck brace for the rest of the show and acting as though he's in constant pain anytime he's near Frank.

before

Southern Belle

When Paige jokes about the layered tulle "petticoat" lampshades that Frank has designed, Frank smugly admits, "During the Civil War, I used to make 'em for the troops."

TCR 01:22.44:2

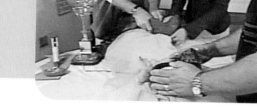

TCR 01:35.42.2

Frank the Vampire Slayer?

During the end credits an extended shot of Frank shows him carving the giant pencil from a piece of unpainted wood. Frank tells the camera that he's making a vampire stake and cautions viewers to be careful whom they stab, because "anyone walking around after dawn is not a vampire."

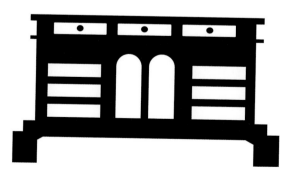

S3
E26

London, England: Garden Flat

$ | **Cast:** Paige, Genevieve, Hildi, Handy Andy | Genevieve's Room: ☺ ☺ ☹ | Hildi's Room: ☺ ☺ ☹

01:38:09.12
after

01:38:07.05
before

DESIGNED BY GENEVIEVE

The Rooms

Gen enlivens a bedroom by painting the walls a rich, spicy orange, painting a small alcove red, and hanging many yellow-green draperies. She also builds a new platform bed with drawers beneath, adds a ready-made dresser, creates closet space along one wall, installs crown molding, and hangs rows of framed Chinese newsprint. Hildi brightens a bedroom shared by two girls by splattering brightly colored paint onto white walls, laying fluffy white carpet, framing the girls' artwork, and sewing rainbow-color draperies. She also installs doors on an existing wall-size shelving unit, builds beds and nightstands on casters, and creates a "secret garden" area with wheatgrass plants.

Dialect Differences
Gen tries to explain the concept of crown molding to Handy Andy, who eventually explains that the British call the same thing "coving."

Notable
This is the first International Challenge between *Trading Spaces* and its British sister show, *Changing Rooms*.

Maybe He's Right
Gen comes upon Handy Andy working on her bed platform with a screwdriver. She asks why he's not using a power tool, and he explains that the "battery's gone flat." Gen starts picking on him for not charging his tools, and he says that she's used to getting nothing but jokes from her carpenters (Ty and Amy Wynn). She says to the camera, "He's an attitude carpenter. ... It's all business out here. Geez."

Hey Look, Kids ... Paige says Time's Up in front of Big Ben.

after

DESIGNED BY HILDI

before

01:37:58.29

Budget Busters

While Gen barely squeaks by, spending exactly $1,000 (or £648) on her room, Hildi is over budget at $1,394.80 (or £894).

Messy Madam

After throwing paint on the walls, Hildi is completely covered in paint (a *Trading Spaces* first?). She apparently didn't remember her own advice to a paint-covered Dez in Lawrenceville: Pine Lane (Season 1, Episode 5): "Delegate, delegate, delegate!"

More Weather Woes

While struggling with the tent, Handy Andy points out that the old slate tiles on nearby roofs may blow off and hit people below. Paige is concerned and decides to move Gen's dresser assembly project inside.

Handy Andy and Paige meet at the end of Day I to discuss the progress of each room.

Weather Woes

Gale-force winds upset the show on Day 2, blowing the Carpentry World tent into a neighboring yard. Gen, Paige, and Handy Andy jump over the neighbor's fence and try to put the tent back into place. After getting it back in the right spot, but not getting it to stand up completely, Handy Andy turns to the two giggling women and dismisses them, saying, "You've annoyed me enough now."

S3

E27

Mississippi: Golden Pond

✳ | **Cast:** Paige, Hildi, Laurie, Amy Wynn | Hildi's Room: ☺ ☹ ☹ | Laurie's Room: ☺ ☹ ☹

after

before

DESIGNED BY LAURIE

The Rooms

Laurie updates a bedroom by painting the walls camel-yellow, building a large headboard of upholstered aqua fabric with a chocolate brown grid overlay, creating a large mirror from smaller mirrored squares, hanging a thrift store chandelier, adding new upholstered thrift store chairs, using aqua and camel-yellow bedding, and building new chocolate brown bookcases. Hildi adds color to a bathroom (a *Trading Spaces* first!) by stapling more than 6,000 silk flowers to the walls, painting the trim and cabinets gold, creating red acrylic cabinet door insets, building a bench upholstered in terry cloth, and sewing draperies and a shower curtain from French floral fabrics.

> **Down and Out:** Laurie removes the existing ceiling fan.

after

before

DESIGNED BY HILDI

For Laughs

Laurie is in high spirits this episode, hula-hooping during a bumper shot, doing her version of a New Jersey accent during the end credits (remember New Jersey: Sam Street (Season 1, Episode 38?), and doing her best impression of an upholstered headboard for her homeowners.

Tub Time

While sitting (apparently naked) in a tub full of bubbles, the bathroom homeowners describe what they'd like to see done to their room.

Notable

This is Laurie's first episode since returning from maternity leave. Baby Gibson makes a quick appearance on the morning of Day 2.

Whew!

At the end of Day 1, Paige and Amy Wynn sneak past the bathroom window where Hildi's homeowners are still stapling flowers to the walls. The two talk about how glad they are that they don't have to stay and help.

S3
E28

Mississippi: Winsmere Way

Cast: Paige, Hildi, Laurie, Amy Wynn

Hildi's Room: ☺ ☺ ☹ | **Laurie's Room:** ☺ ☺ ☹

after

before

Deco-Dramas

The Rooms

Hildi adds drama to a bedroom by covering the walls in red toile fabric, painting the ceiling smoky plum, slipcovering a thrift store sofa with cream fabric, building a new armoire with curved doors, repainting two thrift store lamps, and creating shadow boxes. Laurie spices up the bedroom of a newly divorced homeowner with cumin yellow paint on the walls, an eggplant-color ceiling, a large upholstered headboard with nailhead trim, a new chaise lounge, a blown-glass light fixture, and two upholstered message boards.

Laurie has some stressful moments during the episode. Her purple ceiling isn't quite the eggplant shade she had hoped for (she calls it Disco '70s Nightmare and goes out to find new paint). Later Laurie doesn't have enough ribbon to create her message boards, but her homeowners design a new pattern for the ribbon. Laurie gushes that she's so glad when she has smart homeowners.

Deco-Dramas, Part 2

Laurie's "smart homeowners" have moments of their own, however: While hanging two towel bars that act as magazine racks, they nearly destroy the wall while attempting to install wall anchors and they can't seem to get the racks level. During the end credits, there is a shot of them working on this project, and the male homeowner says that the real-life stuff isn't aired.

after

before

Great Minds Think Alike
Both Laurie and Hildi remove the existing ceiling fans in their rooms.

S3
E29

San Antonio, TX: Ghostbridge

Cast: Paige, Hildi, Vern, Ty

Hildi's Room: ☺ ☺ ☹ | Vern's Room: ☺ ☺ ☹

The Rooms

Hildi gets groovy in a living room by lining one wall with record albums and painting the remaining walls purple, yellow, teal, and orange. She creates slipcovers in the same colors, makes a coffee table top by covering a colorful scarf with a large piece of glass, paints the homeowners' favorite chair black with brightly colored flowers, installs lamps made from French drainpipes, and designs a large entertainment center. Vern leaves his mark in a living room by covering one wall with wood veneer wallpaper, bringing in new pieces of brown furniture, hanging red draperies, creating a red and gold leaf coffee table and room screen, and laying a red rug.

DESIGNED BY HILDI

Happy Feet

When Ty and Hildi's male homeowner bring in the base for the entertainment center, Hildi jumps on it and starts dancing before they've had a chance to put it down.

Notable: Hildi refers to herself as the Slipcover Queen.

Is It Really a Surprise?
Hildi removes the existing ceiling fan. Vern follows suit.

DESIGNED BY VERN

Attraction Action

One of Vern's homeowners has a crush on Vern and Ty. During the episode, she flirts with both of them, protects Vern from criticism, and refers to him as "my Vern."

Reveal-ing Moment

The album room homeowner cries but isn't sure about her room and keeps repeating, "This is ... unique."

S3
E30

Austin, TX: Wyoming Valley Drive

Cast: Paige, Hildi, Laurie, Ty

Hildi's Room: ☺ ☺ ☹ | Laurie's Room: ☺ ☺ ☹

after

TCR 01:38.21:
PLAY   LO

before

TCR 01:38.18:28
PLAY   LOCK

The Rooms

Laurie adds warmth to a dining room by weaving one wall with brown sueded cotton and painting the other walls pink-orange. She builds a round dining table with a stenciled top and a fabric skirt, designs a buffet table with legs made from plumbing conduit, and makes draperies and seat cushions from green fabric. Hildi creates a sleek kitchen by covering the walls with peel-and-stick wine labels, painting the cabinets black, enlarging an existing bench, designing a large pot rack from lumber and copper plumbing conduit, painting the existing wooden blinds black and orange, slipcovering the dining chairs with orange fabric, and embellishing the dining table with gold accents.

Quotable Quotes

Paige asks the dining room homeowners what they're afraid of finding when they return home. The female homeowner says that she doesn't want any type of neon color, and Paige replies sarcastically, "Yeah, because Laurie is known for neon."

after

TCR 01:38.16:29
PLAY   LOCK

Reveal-ing Moment

The kitchen homeowners, who don't drink or keep any type of alcohol in their home, aren't thrilled with the labels. Their neighbors enter the room at the end of the show with a steamer, tied with a ribbon, that can be used to remove the labels.

Coincidence?

While working on their neighbors' kitchen, Hildi's homeowners talk about having to redo anything they don't like about their own room. The female homeowner quietly says, "[We'll be] taking cowhide off the walls." Little does she know that Laurie is creating a faux leather woven wall treatment.

before

TCR 01:38.12:18
PLAY   LOCK

189

S3
E31

Austin, TX: Aire Libre Drive

💧 $ | **Cast:** Paige, Frank, Kia, Ty   Frank's Room: ☺ 😐 ☹ | Kia's Room: ☺ 😐 ☹

The Rooms

Frank adds drama to a living room by painting one wall orange and the other walls yellow, building two new end tables, designing a massive coffee table out of a black granite slab and four decorative columns, adding a toy chest to hold dog toys, covering the existing furniture with multicolor fabric, and laying a new rug. Kia updates a living room by painting the walls moss green and brown, painting a gold-color glaze over the brown paint, designing new draperies from various types of printed fabric, building a large frame above the fireplace, adding a new love seat, and scavenging accessories from other rooms in the house.

DESIGNED BY FRANK

after

before

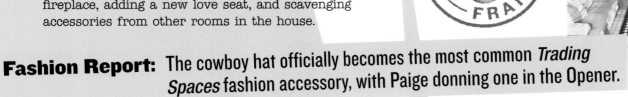

Fashion Report: The cowboy hat officially becomes the most common *Trading Spaces* fashion accessory, with Paige donning one in the Opener.

With This Ring

Frank's male homeowner complains that his wife is the boss, and Frank assures him that he is not alone. Frank displays his wedding ring and talks about how it cuts off the circulation to his brain.

$$

Budget Crisis

Frank is already $123 over budget when his homeowners meet him on Day 1. He manages to return enough items over the course of the show that he's under budget by Designer Chat.

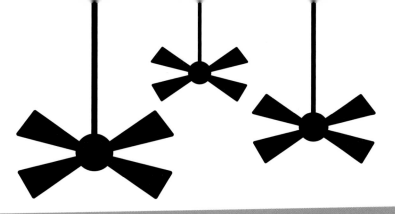

Bye-Bye, Blades! Vern removes an existing ceiling fan.

01:38:25.28

after

DESIGNED BY VERN

Headboard Headaches

Gen's grass-cloth headboard falls apart when Ty and her female homeowner try to move it off a construction table. They have to rebuild it.

01:38:23.08

before

Farm Fetish?
When Gen's homeowners tell her that they're not really worried about what Vern may be doing to their home, Gen jokes that Vern has been wanting to explore new design avenues, including "the barnyard look." Oddly enough, the next scene shows Vern telling his female homeowner to stuff a pillow as she would stuff a turkey.

Tearjerker: Both sets of homeowners love their rooms. The two female homeowners cry at the end.

Sheesh!
Ty shamelessly points out Gen's morning coffee breath on the morning of Day 2.

195

B-Roll

Creating an episode of *Trading Spaces*

can't be all work, can it? No way! At the start of each episode, the cast can be seen hamming it up at a site near where an episode is filmed. The cast has been spotted at casinos, amusement parks, the ocean, racetracks, and beyond. Here's a glimpse at some of the most exciting, funniest B-Roll moments caught on film.

Farm Fun

Doug drives a tractor. Vern and Amy Wynn tractor-surf and put up hay. (Indiana: Fieldhurst Lane, Season 3, Episode 21)

It's Magic!

Gen, Doug, and Ty wear costumes and bad wigs while performing a magic trick. Doug cuts Ty in half with a chain saw while Gen strikes poses. (Austin, TX: Wampton Way, Season 3, Episode 32)

Fast-Food Funnies

Gen playfully puts two large french fries in her mouth as if they were walrus tusks, and Ty jokingly tries to stuff one into his nose. (Los Angeles, CA: Elm Street, Season 3, Episode 48)

Play Ball!

Edward pitches, Doug bats, and Carter catches while at a baseball field. (South Carolina: Sherborne Drive, Season 3, Episode 56)

Indy Excitement

Edward drives an an Indy car with Kia as his passenger, and Amy Wynn waves the checkered flag. This is Kia's favorite B-Roll moment! (Indiana: Halleck Way, Season 3, Episode 22)

196

Dreams DO Come True!

Amy Wynn, Hildi, and Frank are at the Magic Kingdom and are photographed with Minnie Mouse and Pluto. Hildi is one of Pluto's biggest fans—and meeting him was a *Trading Spaces* highlight! (Whisper Lake, FL: Season 3, Episode 54)

Ouch!

Gen and Amy Wynn watch as a tattoo artist "inks" a fake tattoo *Trading Spaces* logo onto Laurie's bicep. (Los Angeles, CA: Murietta Avenue, Season 3, Episode 37)

A Blissful Union?

Hildi and Doug go to a drive-in marriage chapel in a convertible where Amy Wynn officiates. (Las Vegas, NV: Carlsbad Caverns, Season 3, Episode 40)

Ouch 2!

Gen bounces a basketball off her head as if it were a soccer ball. Doug looks concerned and kisses her forehead. (Indiana: River Valley Drive, Season 3, Episode 20)

S3
E34

California: Dusty Trail

Cast: Paige, Doug, Genevieve, Ty | **Doug's Room:** ☺ ☺ ☹ | **Genevieve's Room:** ☺ ☺ ☹

The Rooms

Doug designs a bedroom he calls Cosmo Shab by colorwashing the walls with three shades of blue paint, painting the cathedral ceiling gray, installing crown molding, hanging a chandelier removed from the dining room, sewing gray and white toile draperies, painting the existing furniture white, and distressing the newly painted pieces to create an antique look. Gen transforms a kitchen into a French *boucherie* (butcher shop) by covering the walls with green chalkboard paint, painting the cabinets vanilla with gray insets, installing a tin ceiling, building a larger tabletop, and hanging pictures of "meat puppets" around the room.

after

DESIGNED BY DOUG

before

New Toy
Doug and Ty have fun with a new piece of equipment—a laser-pointer level that is the size of a large tape measure.

MAKEUP!
While working on the blue colorwash, Doug's male homeowner accidentally gets blue paint all over Paige's eyelid.

Quotable Quote
When the female bedroom homeowner sees her room, she says, "I feel so bad for saying all that bad stuff about Doug!"

Fashion Report: The cast members wear wet suits, and Ty successfully surfs.

Pearly Whites
Paige tells Doug's female homeowner, "You have perfect teeth." Doug is disappointed that Paige doesn't say the same about his teeth and jokingly pouts.

> He might have a lot of attitude, but he's a damn fine designer.
> —Gen praises Doug

after

Tardy Tin

The tin for Gen's ceiling doesn't arrive until the morning of Day 2. Because Ty has to work on Doug's room, Gen's male homeowner installs the tin himself. For The Reveal, most of the tin is installed, with the exception of a small strip at the edge of the room. Gen informs viewers, "Tin is not a two-day project, just so you know."

DESIGNED BY GENEVIE

before

BABY BOOM

As she hands a respirator mask to her pregnant female homeowner, Gen says, "This paint is a little bit toxic, and I want your baby to be born with all its fingers and toes."

She then cites Ty as an example of what could happen to the woman's child if she doesn't wear a mask.

> Ooh la la, my room rocks!
> —Gen

199

S3
E35

California: Fairfield

◊ ☝ ⑦ | **Cast:** Paige, Frank, Kia, Ty | Frank's Room: ☺ 😐 ☹ | Kia's Room: ☺ 😐 ☹

The Rooms

Kia updates an office/game room by painting the walls apricot and the trim orange. She builds a love seat that sits 8 inches off the ground, designs a removable tabletop for an existing game table, builds storage cubes that double as seats, hangs a "mirror" made of CDs, makes chess pieces from copper pipe, and rearranges the existing desk to create a more effective office area. Frank designs a "tranquil love nest" in a bedroom, adding coffee-color paint, a new coffee bar (complete with a small refrigerator), wooden chevrons on the existing furniture, gauzy fabric draped around the four-poster bed, and a large piece of bamboo for a drapery rod.

after

DESIGNED BY KIA

01:38:06.27.2

01:38:04.04.2

before

Wise Words
Frank encourages his male homeowner while they're stuffing pillows by saying, "Become one with your batting."

Tearjerker: The bedroom homeowners cry happy tears upon seeing their room.

Watch Your Step
Frank's male homeowner bought new shoes for the show but steps in a full paint tray early in Day I.

after

01:37:57.15.2

DESIGNED BY FRANK

before

Stress Alert!
Kia's window treatment plan is a fiasco: The blinds must be dismantled, and the slats have to be hand-numbered (there are more than 150 slats), covered with spray adhesive, and attached to a piece of fabric. Each slat is then supposed to be cut apart and restrung so that either the fabric side or the copper side is exposed. Midway through Day 2, Kia's male homeowner has completed only one full blind and a portion of the second. Because the project doesn't turn out as planned, in the end the room is void of window coverings.

Mirror, Mirror
Paige asks whether Kia expects the homeowners to be able to see themselves in the CD "mirror" she designed. Kia and Paige debate the reflectiveness of the CDs until Kia finally looks at herself in a CD and says, "I'm a little distorted and very prismed, but I can see myself clearly."

S3 E36

San Diego, CA: Duenda Road

Cast: Paige, Frank, Vern, Amy Wynn

Frank's Room: ☺ 😐 ☹ | Vern's Room: ☺ 😐 ☹

after

TCR 01:39.06:18
PLAY L

DESIGNED BY FRANK

The Rooms

Frank adds romance to a bedroom by painting the walls soft green, building a canopy frame from molding strips, hanging a gauzy canopy from the ceiling, and revamping an existing dresser. Vern updates a living room by painting the walls with two tones of soft green, surrounding the existing fireplace with slate tiles, painting the existing furniture a third shade of green, hanging glass vases on the wall, installing green chenille draperies, and creating a new entertainment center.

before

TCR 01:39.04:13
PLAY LOCK

Quotable Frank

Frank-isms abound in this episode. Some highlights: When his female homeowner has difficulty painting, "You don't have to strangle the roller, Mary. The roller is your friend." When a homeowner says that Frank's body is in the way of something the homeowner needs to see, Frank retorts, "My body's in the way of the entire wall!"

after

TCR 01:39.02:09
PLAY LOCK

Aquatic Antics
Most of the B-Roll footage for the episode shows the cast hanging out at SeaWorld. Frank kisses a dolphin (he says swimming with dolphins is his favorite B-Roll memory), Paige talks to killer whales, Vern rides a dolphin, and Amy Wynn has all sorts of adorable escapades with a seal and a sea otter.

DESIGNED BY VERN

before

TCR 01:38.58:16
PLAY LOCK

"You can't spend money to buy time."
—Paige to Vern during Designer Chat

Devotion to Detail

Vern's female homeowner tells him that his drawing of the fireplace tile layout is "like a science project."

S3
E37

Los Angeles, CA: Murietta Avenue

$ | **Cast:** Paige, Genevieve, Laurie, Amy Wynn | **Genevieve's Room:** ☺ ☺ ☹ | **Laurie's Room:** ☺ ☺ ☹

The Rooms

Gen gives a bland living/dining room a 1940s L.A. twist by painting the walls dark red, painting the trim bright white, adding white crown molding, and hanging draperies featuring a palm frond print. Gen also designs lighted display shelves, frames book illustrations of L.A. in the 1940s, reupholsters the dining room chairs with more palm frond fabrics, and hangs a new period light fixture. Laurie creates a warm and comfortable living room by painting the walls butter yellow, with bands of golden camel and cream near the top of the walls. She installs built-in wall cabinets to house electronic equipment and "hideaway dog beds," lays a large khaki area rug, paints the fireplace white, slipcovers the sofa, and adds two green chenille chairs.

after

before

Respect for the Dead

As Gen cleans off a cluttered entertainment center shelf, she encounters the cremated remains of two dogs, stored in boxes with little dog statues on top of them. She makes several uncomfortable faces as she picks them up and hands them to her homeowners.

Guns N' Stitches

Slash (of Guns N' Roses fame, who's good friends with Gen's homeowner) hangs out with Gen and the homeowner in Sewing World. Gen tells Slash to sit down and learn to sew too. He does.

Sorry, Gen

Gen jokingly contrasts her design style with Laurie's, claiming Laurie always manages to delegate tasks. Gen then assumes a Southern accent and says, "Y'all, it's time to paint." Yet somehow, Gen still gets stuck doing the painting.

Ouch!
During the Opener, Gen and Amy Wynn watch as a tattoo artist "inks" the *Trading Spaces* logo onto Laurie's bicep.

after

before

DESIGNED BY LAURIE

Southern Charm
Laurie finds out on Day 2 that the carpet she ordered won't arrive for two more days. As a result, she and Paige go shopping and find a carpet Laurie likes. When Laurie asks the very nice carpet salesman (who happens to be friends with Gen's male homeowner whose room Laurie is redoing) if the carpet is in her price range (she can spend only $45), he does some quick calculations with a calculator and says, "We're gonna make it in your price range." Laurie hugs him.

Budget Buster
Laurie winds up over budget.

Notable
The end credits feature a long shot of everyone (and we mean everyone) doing a kick line.

TX E100S 18

Musical Moment
Paige dances and spray-paints dining chairs while Gen's male homeowner plays polka music on an accordion.

Rock On!: Gen's male homeowner is a guitarist; he has toured with Alice Cooper, Slash, Guns N' Roses, and Carole King.

S3

E38

Scottsdale, AZ: Bell Road

💧 ◄ㅣ▮ | **Cast:** Paige, Frank, Vern, Ty | Frank's Room: ☺ 😐 ☹ | Vern's Room: ☺ 😐 ☹

The Rooms ••••••••

Frank adds a touch of whimsy to a girl's bedroom by painting geometric shapes on the walls with different shades of pastel paints; painting different sections of the walls purple; installing a desk unit that looks like a monkey; laying a multicolor rug; designing a doll-inspired TV cabinet; and adding blue beanbag chairs, multicolored linens, and large throw pillows. Vern creates a soothingly sexy bedroom by painting two walls deep purple, covering two walls and the ceiling with maple planks, building a birch platform bed, installing a cable lighting fixture, hanging mirrored candle sconces throughout the room, designing a long entertainment/storage bench, and recovering an existing sofa with dark purple fabric.

after

DESIGNED BY FRANK

Tell the Truth

When the two sets of homeowners come together at the end, one female homeowner asks the other, "Do you hate us for the monkey?"

before

> **Every little girl needs a monkey in her room.**
> —Frank

Feathered Friends

Frank's homeowners have two birds (Cinnamon and Yoko) that make several appearances during the episode. After they squawk through the Key Swap, Paige says, "Those birds are gonna be the end of me," and walks off camera tweeting. On the morning of Day 2, the homeowners meet Frank in front of the house and reveal that there were "heat problems" with the house, so they stayed at a hotel—taking the birds along. While painting the face for the TV cabinet, Frank has one bird on his shoulder and another on his head. After talking to the birds about his project, Frank suspects that one has relieved itself on his head. He says, "Isn't it just like life? You work and you work and you work and … a bird poops on you."

Tearjerker: The female maple plank bedroom homeowner cries tears of joy.

Bedtime Story

During Designer Chat, Vern tells Paige, "To me that's what this room is all about. The remarkable story of the maple and the wood and the whole journey to get to this finished product."

after

before

Risk Taker

When discussing his design plans with Ty, Vern says, "Everything in this room is gonna be very Zen, very sleek, clean, minimal lines." Ty dryly says, "That's pretty new for you, isn't it?"

Use What's Handy: Ty suns himself with a metal dustpan.

Monkeyin' Around

Frank tells Ty to let his creativity flow while making the desk; Ty decides to build it in the shape of a large monkey face. The mouth flips down on hinges to be the main workspace, and the eyes flip down to be a shelf. There are many discussions about whether or not it matches the theme of the room. The desk stays, but at The Reveal the girl's mother doesn't realize what the piece is right away and exclaims, "You have a bar!"

S3 E39 Scottsdale, AZ: Windrose Avenue

💧 ❋ | **Cast:** Paige, Doug, Frank, Ty | Doug's Room: ☺ ☺ ☹ | Frank's Room: ☺ ☺ ☹

The Rooms

Doug transforms a large bedroom into two intimate areas by building a large I-shape wall in the center of the room: He places the existing bed on one side of the wall and places a sofa and armoire removed from other rooms in the house on the other side of the wall. He also paints the existing walls yellow, the new wall rust red, sews new rust and yellow bedding with mod square embellishments, designs a plank-style coffee table, and hangs two of the homeowners' favorite tulip paintings on each side of the wall. Frank transports a bedroom to India during the Colonial period by painting the walls deep purple, reusing the existing navy drapes, adding a navy valance with gold stenciling, dividing the room from the bathroom by hanging white sheets stenciled with a filigree pattern in brown paint, creating nightstands from inverted bamboo trash cans, adding lamps with beaded shades, and converting an existing dresser into a TV armoire.

after

before

DESIGNED BY DOUG

Boys Will Be Boys

When the homeowners enter, Doug and Ty are playing football in the bedroom, catching passes by falling on the bed.

Low Riders

Ty's pants begin to sag dangerously low while he's working on Doug's wall. Paige (wearing safety goggles) hikes his pants back up and says, "I wish these were sunglasses!" and leaves the room. Ty calls after her, "Need a little caulk in that crack!"

DESIGNED BY FRANK

" To me, a bedroom is supposed to have a lot of pillows.

—Frank's design advice "

after

before

Yawn

Frank says to his homeowners, "How many times have you told yourself, 'I wish I weren't here. I wish I was out sewing somewhere'?" Once he and his male homeowner are sewing pillows, Frank's bored and says, "I am pulsating with excitement."

Fan Ban: Doug removes the existing ceiling fan.

Tearjerker: The female purple bedroom homeowner cries.

Remember When?

Doug tells his homeowner that the existing armoire isn't his cup of tea by saying, "Somebody said to me once in an episode, 'I see a bunch of firewood.'" He's referring to Seattle: 137th Street (Season 2, Episode 21).

The Name Game
Doug names his room Barrier. He later jokes that he should have called it Racetrack because the homeowners' kids will chase each other in circles around it.

S3
E40

Vegas, NV: Carlsbad Caverns

Cast: Paige, Doug, Hildi, Amy Wynn   **Doug's Room:** ☺ ☺ ☹   **Hildi's Room:** ☺ ☺ ☹

The Rooms

To redecorate a living room, Hildi draws inspiration from a painting she bought in London. She paints the walls burgundy, paints the ceiling sky blue, adds six burgundy columns throughout the room, lays checkerboard vinyl flooring in two shades of orange, hangs burgundy draperies, and upholsters furniture and stitches pillows in every shade of the rainbow. Doug covers the walls of a bedroom in dark brown Venetian plaster. He paints the ceiling peach, hangs bright blue draperies, sews pillows and bedding in various blue fabrics, installs crown molding, builds a large round white armoire, and creates a four-poster look around the existing bed with four alleged stripper poles.

after

before

Fan Phobic

Hildi removes the existing ceiling fan in her room.

Designer Favorites

Hildi praises Doug's room: She says her favorite room designed by a fellow castmate "has to be Doug's blue bedroom with the stripper poles."

Thread-Bare

On the morning of Day 2, Hildi discovers that the fabric she shipped isn't going to arrive in time. She goes speed-shopping for fabric and must sew everything in one afternoon.

Ouch!

When Paige asks Doug what color he painted the ceiling in his room, he replies, "Blush," and playfully slaps her cheeks to show her the color.

Notable: The Reveals for this episode originally aired live.

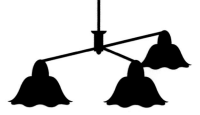

Take That!

When Doug's male homeowner complains about painting the ceiling peach, Doug harasses him by asking what color the carpet is in his house. The carpet is pink, so Doug tells the homeowner that because of his carpet color, he doesn't get a say in color choices.

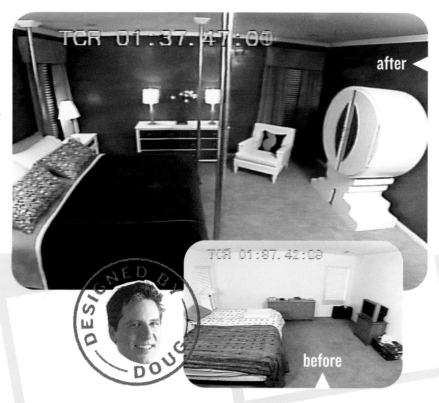

after

before

Happy Couple?

During the Opener, Hildi and Doug go to a drive-through wedding chapel where Amy Wynn officiates. After Amy Wynn ominously says, "You are wed," Hildi and Doug kiss. Hildi pulls away and says, "Stop opening your mouth!" Doug looks coyly into the camera and shrugs his shoulders.

Fame Game

Vegas celebs aplenty in this episode! Robin Leach presents Doug and his team with champagne and compliments them on upping the style in their homes; using a drill, Penn & Teller perform a card trick for Amy Wynn; Rita Rudner does the splits; and an Elvis impersonator helps Doug hang valances while singing "Amazing Paint." Only in Vegas, baby, only in Vegas.

Vegas, NV: Smokemont Courts

S3
E41

Cast: Paige, Edward, Laurie, Amy Wynn

Edward's Room: ☺ ☺ ☹ | Laurie's Room: ☺ ☺ ☹

The Rooms

Edward designs a hip, funky office with one purple wall. He paints the remaining walls and ceiling light gray, constructs a large black built-in desk, designs black shelving, uses the homeowner's guitars as artwork, creates window shades from plastic sheets and paper clips, drapes white fabric across one wall, and incorporates a gray flannel chaise lounge. Laurie updates a bland living room by painting the walls taupe, building a large square shelving unit, painting the shelving insets coral, laying a large brown area rug, hanging conduit piping as drapery rods, hanging an upholstered piece of fabric as artwork, utilizing the existing black love seats, adding a square coffee table, and converting an existing side table into an ottoman.

after

before

Purple Passion

On first seeing Edward's purple paint, his female homeowner exclaims, "The purple is not good!" When Paige stops by to check their progress, she finds the female homeowner painting shapes and letters on the wall as her husband diligently works beside her. Paige asks why she's goofing off, and she tries to prove she's working hard by placing Paige's hand in her armpit to see how sweaty she is. Later Paige finds her painting the ceiling gray instead of finishing the purple wall because she doesn't want to have to take responsibility for the color if her neighbors hate it.

Switch to Decaf

Edward's female homeowner is quite a character. After Edward explains the window shade project, she asks, "Do I do this before or after my nap?" When Edward stops by to see how she and Paige are coming on the shades, she quickly points fingers and says, "Paige is slow!" When Edward grabs the silver spray paint and paints a clear plate, she quickly asks, "I hope that wasn't crystal. Was that crystal? Did that look like crystal to you?!" Paige deadpans, "Who's Crystal?"

after

Point Taken

Laurie starts to show her male homeowner how she wants her lampshades spray-painted. After she's nearly completed one of the two shades, the homeowner points out, "You're not really delegating as much as you are demonstrating."

before

Seating Switcheroo

Laurie plans to swap the existing black sofas with portions of a taupe sectional found in another room of the house. There is much discussion about leaving them with only a corner portion of the sectional and two black love seats in a separate room, and the female homeowner asks, "We take one hodgepodge and turn it into another hodgepodge?" When Laurie realizes she can't take the sectional apart in the way she hoped, the male homeowner says, "This is where the drama comes in." Laurie laments, "This means that my absolute plan is foiled."

Win Some, Lose Some

During B-Roll footage, Laurie and Edward play roulette, while Amy Wynn runs the table. When they lose money on their bet, Laurie says, "There went my lamps."

SHOCKER!

When Laurie tells her team she's leaving the existing ceiling fan in the room, her male homeowner exclaims, "This isn't *Trading Spaces!*"

Reveal-ing Moment

This is one of the more memorable *Trading Spaces* Reveals. Edward's female homeowner was very adamant at the start of the show that she did not want brown in her finished room. Not realizing that, Laurie designed a room that was primarily taupe. Upon opening her eyes, the homeowner keeps saying things like, "I hate brown ... I hate the orange and brown!" and "I'm trying to be a big person. We won't do brown!" When her neighbors come in and begin apologizing, she starts shoving the other female homeowner, shouting, "We promised!" and makes a dramatic exit through the front door. During the end credits, there's a shot of her taking the other female homeowner down in a headlock and Paige trying to break them up.

S3
E42

Vegas, NV: Woodmore Court

Cast: Paige, Genevieve, Vern, Amy Wynn

Genevieve's Room: ☺ ☺ ☹ | Vern's Room: ☺ ☺ ☹

The Rooms

Gen goes bold in a living room by painting plant ledges in various shades of purple, building a dark wooden surround for the fireplace and TV cabinet, hanging two raspberry-shape light fixtures, painting a stained-glass treatment on the windows, designing a square coffee table with an inset basket center filled with floating candles, and hanging long white linen curtains. Vern re-creates the feel of a breezy summer day in a living room by painting light yellow 1-foot-wide stripes across the walls, building a large white armoire, adding doors that match the armoire to an existing wall niche, slipcovering the existing furniture with blue fabric, transforming two thrift store computer desks into a square coffee table, and installing white crown molding.

Nail Noshing
While working on one of Vern's pieces, Amy Wynn holds nails in her mouth as she's working. With her mouth full, she mumbles, "Don't do this at home."

Versatile Vern
Paige breaks one of the arms on Vern's new chandelier as she's installing it. When Vern comes to see how it looks, his male homeowner tries to help cover Paige's mistake and spins it around to show him the good side. Vern laughs and says, "My powers of perception go beyond simple rotation!"

Why? Vern's female homeowner wears fake buck teeth the morning of Day 2.

Shear Perfection
There's a shot of Paige joking with Vern while measuring his paint stripes during the end credits. She sarcastically asks him how long the spikes in his hair are. Without missing a beat, Vern replies, "$2\frac{3}{16}$ inches."

S3	
E43	

Miami, FL: Ten Court

☻ ⑤ | **Cast:** Paige, Hildi, Kia, Ty   Hildi's Room: ☺ ☺ ☹ | Kia's Room: ☺ ☺ ☹

after

before

The Rooms

Hildi adds an art gallery look to a living room with periwinkle blue walls, a slipcovered thrift store sofa to match the walls, a new brick paver floor, a wooden-slat bench-style coffee table, track lighting, and canvases covered in several pastel paints blended into one another. Kia heads toward the sea in a bedroom with a shell-shape head- and footboard, sea-blue walls, bedside shelves made from bamboo, window shades made with fabric stretched across a bamboo frame, a wide wallpaper border, and a seagrass rug.

Cabinet Crisis

Kia designs a TV cabinet with framed mirrors as doors. The large decorative frames and mirrors are too heavy, and the cabinet tips, breaking the mirrors. So, Kia cuts the TV cabinet but uses the frames: One is hung on the wall, framing a note that reads, "We are sorry," and the other is used as a tray to hold candles.

Budget Buster: Hildi's minimalist living room puts her $40.24 over budget.

Paddle Swap?

The two homes are located on a small lake. The homeowners swap keys while sitting in canoes as Paige stands on a dock. After switching keys the homeowners paddle to each other's homes.

after

before

S3
E44

Miami, FL: Miami Place

✳ ☻ $ | **Cast:** Paige, Hildi, Laurie, Ty | Hildi's Room: ☺ ☺ ☹ | Laurie's Room: ☺ ☺ ☹

after

before

The Rooms

Hildi sees spots in a large living room by upholstering several pieces of furniture with cream fabric covered in white and black circles, painting the walls to match the fabric, building a circular shelving unit/entertainment center, repairing existing water damage on the walls, hanging matchstick blinds, and laying a new khaki carpet. Laurie warms a bland living room by painting the walls gold, creating a molding design on the ceiling, hanging a square light fixture, constructing a large built-in cabinet for the big-screen TV, creating a seating area and a dining area, and designing a Hans Hofmann-inspired painting for the new dining area.

Homeowner Fun

The homeowners spray Silly String at each other during the Key Swap, Hildi's female homeowner wears Tweety Bird slippers throughout the episode, and Laurie's female homeowner discusses what Hildi may be doing in her home by saying, "I think she already understands that we don't want anything on the wall except paint."

Stress Alert!

Hildi's entertainment center was originally designed to have four sections that fit together to form a circle. Ty builds the piece, but the sections are too big to fit through the door of the room. He has to rip them down to a smaller size—essentially having to remake each piece. He runs out of time and only has three completed by the end of Day 2.

Hildi hand-paints a portion of a wall to mimic her chosen fabric.

214

after

before

Abracadabra

Laurie reveals her fabric swatch (from which she based the room's color scheme) as a sleight-of-hand magic trick.

Problem Solved!

When the glass shade of the light fixture Laurie plans to use in the room accidentally breaks, she replaces it with a small square light she prefers.

Kicked to the Curb: Laurie removes the existing ceiling fan.

Above and Beyond

Ty discovers a section of wall in Hildi's room that has been severely damaged by water. He has to rip out the damaged Sheetrock, install new wall supports, remove the damaged insulation, and hang new Sheetrock. Hildi points out, "This is way beyond our call of duty." At the other house Paige tells Laurie's homeowners (who own the water-damaged room), "It's a really good thing you guys are really nice people!"

> **I lost this one in '83!**
> —Ty finding a cassette tape while working on the water-damaged wall

SNEAK PEEK

During their Reveals, both female homeowners tell their husbands to open their eyes first.

Budget Busters

Hildi's unexpected water damage repairs put her over budget by $2.49. Laurie's new light fixture sent her just a touch over budget; she spends 26 cents too much.

S3
E45

Miramar, FL: Avenue 164

💧 $ | **Cast:** Paige, Doug, Frank, Ty | Doug's Room: ☺ ☺ ☹ | Frank's Room: ☺ ☺ ☹

The Rooms

Doug energizes a bland, white kitchen by painting the walls citron green and the cabinets tomato red, adding concentric rectangles to the cabinet fronts with molding, replacing some drawers with dark brown wicker baskets, and adding several brightly colored plants in white pots throughout the room. Frank looks to the future in a bedroom by painting the walls deep red, building a headboard out of various upholstered shapes, sewing a duvet cover from vintage fabric, painting the existing furniture black, hanging long black doors around the room as artwork, and designing a large black, futuristically styled entertainment center.

after

before

DESIGNED BY DOUG

> ## "Have people not learned that these are not good taste?"
> **—Doug on refrigerator magnets**

Wiggle Room

Trying to save money on his budget, Doug takes dirt out of an existing outdoor potted plant for his kitchen flowers. Paige starts planting the new flowers unaware of the dirt's origins. As she starts grabbing dirt by the handful she becomes confused and says, "There's worms in here, Doug."

The Name Game: Paige names Doug's room Contempo-ribbean Kitchen.

Frank dons a sequined rubber-chicken tie, which he proudly displays during his Designer Chat.

DESIGNED BY FRANK

after

before

You Said It!

After seeing Frank's design drawings, Ty tells him, "You've switched out folk for funk!"

SIZE Matters

Frank's room is so large that he's spreading bread crumbs through it when he first meets his homeowners so that they can find their way around. Later Paige says that the bedroom and adjoining master bathroom are bigger than her Manhattan apartment. Frank responds, "It's bigger than my town."

TX E100S 18   TX E100S 19
18A   18   19A   19

Three-Alarm Blaze

Doug's team accidentally trips the fire alarm in the kitchen, and the fire department is automatically called. As a fire truck pulls up outside with sirens blaring, Paige walks up to meet it. She apologizes and explains the situation. When a fireman asks if they should still check things out, she jokingly says, "You can take a look if you want, but, really, it's just because we're idiots."

Crikey!

During the Opener, Paige rides on a fan boat through the Florida Everglades. Later she holds a small alligator during a bumper shot.

Tearjerker

When the two sets of homeowners come together in the end, the women start crying happy tears, and everyone's reaching quickly to hug each other, knocking Paige backward in the melee.

Budget Buster

Frank's large room required a large budget; he's 85 cents over the spending limit.

S3 E46 Orlando, FL: Smith Street

✳ $ | **Cast:** Paige, Hildi, Kia, Amy Wynn | Hildi's Room: ☺ ☺ ☹ | Kia's Room: ☺ ☺ ☹

The Rooms

Hildi helps reorganize the space in an efficiency apartment by painting the walls mango, building a large bed unit that can be used as a king-size bed or divided so the homeowner's daughter has her own space when she visits, making a roll screen from her own photo of the Arc d'Triomphe to divide the bed, adding a dining/entertaining area with thrift store tables and chairs, reconfiguring the closet storage to include a desk area, and painting the carpet brown. Kia remakes a bedroom in a Moroccan theme by painting the walls green; hanging purple, green, and gold draperies; adding a copper glaze to the ceiling; building a large headboard with a Moroccan-motif cutout; hanging wallpaper "columns" on the wall; and switching the existing closet doors with mirrored ones.

Hey!

Amy Wynn writes several measurements on the white, unpainted wall to help her install the new headboard. She writes "No paint zone" in large letters and explains to the homeowners that they shouldn't paint over that part of the wall. Soon after, Hildi reveals her paint colors by rolling them on the wall—right over Amy Wynn's measurements. Amy Wynn exclaims, "What's that 'No paint zone' mean to you?"

Exotic Breezes: Kia adds a ceiling fan to her Moroccan bedroom design.

Budget Buster

Hildi is $36.29 over budget. During Designer Chat she hands Paige $50 and tells her to keep the change.

S3

E47

Florida: Night Owl Lane

⟶ ⑤ | **Cast:** Paige, Edward, Hildi, Amy Wynn   Edward's Room: ☺ ☺ ☹ | Hildi's Room: ☺ ☺ ☹

after

before

Sour Note

At the end of Day 2, Hildi and her team begin to push the homeowners' Depression-era family heirloom piano back into the room. They make it only a couple of inches when the legs break. Several crew members can be heard yelling "Stop!" and one dives into the shot to help. Later, on the PaigeCam, Amy Wynn explains that repairing the piano is a simple process, but Paige is concerned about whether there is enough time to fix it. Hildi tells Paige that she's overriding her authority and allowing Amy Wynn to do anything she needs to do to fix the problem. Amy Wynn high-fives Hildi and says, "Anarchy, baby!"

The Rooms

Edward adds Eastern flair to a bedroom by painting the walls yellow; designing a headboard with decoratively framed bulletin boards and a footboard with stylized feet; installing two bedside tables mounted to the wall; painting a piece of custom artwork of a Buddha image; antiquing a thrift store dresser, mirror, and bench; hanging brown lambrequins on the windows; and hanging white curtains stenciled with brown henna-style markings to disguise the dressing area. Hildi streamlines a large art collection in a living room by building a new wall with several large shelves to display paintings, texturing the walls with stucco, laying a parquet floor, and changing the furniture configuration.

Language Barrier

While Edward copies Chinese characters from a crafts stencil onto his Buddha painting, Paige tells him she hopes he's not writing anything with a negative sentiment. He double-checks the stencil and assures her it means "luck" and "love."

DESIGNED BY EDWARD

DESIGNED BY HILDI

before

Budget Buster: Hildi's over budget.

Los Angeles, CA: Elm Street

S3
E48

★ | **Cast:** Paige, Genevieve, Vern, Ty

Genevieve's Room: ☺ ☺ ☹ | Vern's Room: ☺ ☺ ☹

The Rooms

Gen updates Sarah Rue's office by painting the walls smoky taupe and the trim brown, building a mahogany L-shape corner desk out of two doors and two oxidized filing cabinets, designing a banquette/lounge seating area, adding red decorative accents, and displaying framed line drawings of cats created by her team. Vern adds warmth to Andy Dick's kitchen and breakfast nook by painting the walls two different shades of terra-cotta, installing a faux terra-cotta tile floor and a brown tile countertop, adding wrought-iron hardware and decorative accents, painting a graphic circular image across several canvases, and sewing rust-tone Roman shades.

after

before

Reveal-ing Moment
Sarah's disappointed when she sees her redecorated office and describes the wall color as "a garbage can kind of gray."

Notable: Sarah Rue and Andy Dick are two of the stars of the TV show *Less Than Perfect*.

Andy's custom artwork for the room.

Oh No You Don't
Several times throughout the episode Andy tells his team, Paige, and Ty that he's tired and needs to "take a quick five." He says it so often the entire end credits segment is a montage of him saying the phrase.

Can He Do That?
Near the end of Day 2, Andy tells Ty that he doesn't want to help install things in Gen's room and calls his assistant, Drew, to take his place. He gives Drew a *Trading Spaces* smock, introduces him to Ty, reminds him "when you look good, I look good," and leaves to "take a quick five."

Fashion Report

Andy insists on cutting the bottom off of his *Trading Spaces* smock so that it bares his midriff. The gag continues through several scenes, including one in which he is upset that he got paint on his shirt and wants a new one. Gen laughs and says, "You can go naked or you can wear that shirt." He chooses the former and removes his shirt. He tries to reattach his microphone by clipping it to his chest. Gen laughs and gives him a piece of tape to stick the mike to his chest. He then does several poses for the camera.

Ick!

Before Vern's team can start painting, the room has to be scrubbed. When Paige asks Sarah why it took so long, she says that the dirt on the walls was so thick it was three-dimensional.

Mundane Minutia

Ty and Vern spend a long time debating the measurement for the countertop facing. The disagreement is over $\frac{1}{16}$ of an inch.

Quotable Quotes

Gen to Andy on her design plans: "I know you think that we just have a hot glue gun and some chintz fabric, but that's not the case." After Andy keeps trying to get out of work, Gen turns to his teammate and knowingly says, "You're the workhorse; he's the showboat." When Andy fools around and rolls primer onto Paige's pants, Gen turns to the camera and says, "No more celebrity episodes!" While painting the filing cabinets, Gen explains, "We're gonna turn this into a rusty delight." When Andy tries to get out of doing homework, Gen tells him, "I don't care what show you're on. You're doin' some homework."

Gen covers Andy's mouth with a piece of tape.

221

S3
E49

Santa Monica, CA: Ocean Park

(?) ($) | **Cast:** Paige, Laurie, Vern, Ty   **Laurie's Room:** ☺ ☺ ☹ | **Vern's Room:** ☺ ☺ ☹

after

The Rooms

Laurie unifies a living room by painting the walls yellow, adding a ready-made desk, hanging Gottlieb-inspired paintings on either side of the fireplace, building out the existing fireplace with a new mantel, laying a new area rug, installing wall shelves, and adding horseshoe-shape chairs. Vern designs a meditative look in a bedroom by painting the walls light blue, building a large white headboard with a square inset shelf to hold a Buddha statue, installing a large entertainment center/shelving unit, adding two bedside tables, and hanging a silver-leaf candle shelf.

DESIGNED BY LAURIE

Gimme, Gimme, Gimme!

As Vern and Laurie are waiting together for their completed carpentry projects, Ty drives up in the *Trading Spaces* pickup. He opens the back to start unloading, and Laurie doesn't see any of her projects. Ty explains, "It's like Christmas, only every present is for Vern."

before

Canvas Com-"moo"-tion

Laurie paints two white canvases with black amoeba-like circles. Paige voices concern that they look like cow hides. Laurie sponges the wall color on the white areas of the canvas, but then she's told they look like Swiss cheese. Laurie explains to Paige that they're inspired by the artist Gottlieb, who painted various organic shapes. Paige asks, "Is poop organic, because this is so crappy?" Laurie tries to explain her choice by saying, "This is supposed to evoke question." Paige falls to the ground laughing and says, "I have a question. Do we have to put it in the room?" Laurie's female homeowner tries to persuade her to ditch the art by saying, "I love you, but I cannot appreciate Gottlieb." Laurie puts her foot down by keeping the pieces in the room and saying, "Art stands alone."

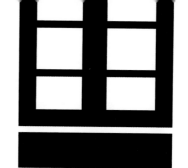

" So you're gonna take his $5,000 bed and replace it with this?

—Vern's homeowner questions Vern's headboard design "

after

DESIGNED BY VERN

Quotable Quote

Paige, Vern, and Vern's team move large carpentry projects into the condo by wheeling them around on dollies. Paige starts dancing and singing, slowing up the process and causing Vern to exclaim, "This is not *Hello Dolly*. You're just using a dolly!"

before

TX E100S 18

18

Fear Factor

One of Vern's female homeowners (the two girls are roommates) is terrified of the staple and nail guns. Every time one goes off, she jumps and giggles hysterically.

Adoration

Vern arrives the morning of Day 1 to find his homeowners have pinned his photograph to their shirts. They have named themselves the Vernettes.

223

S3 E50

Los Angeles, CA: Irving Street

$ | **Cast:** Paige, Frank, Genevieve, Ty | Frank's Room: ☺ ☺ ☹ | Genevieve's Room: ☺ ☺ ☹

The Rooms

Frank adds a modern twist to a bachelor's living room by painting the walls sky blue, adding black and taupe paint to the fireplace, buying all new furniture and lamps, building a wood bar, framing a black and white string art project, and hanging several of the homeowner's photos. Gen looks to orchids for color inspiration in a living room and paints the walls white and the trim green, installs green molding on the curved ceiling, builds a low-slung sofa and a new dining table, and hangs three line drawings of orchids.

after

before

DESIGNED BY FRANK

DESIGNED BY GENEVIEVE

before

after

Budget Buster

Frank's over budget—but only by $9. He gives Paige a $10 bill and says the extra buck is her tip.

Rebel Without a Couch

At the start of the episode, Frank declares that he's significantly over budget and he doesn't care. He tells his homeowners, "I'm getting this surge of power from [being] over budget." Midway through Day 2, Frank's still over budget, and his male homeowner encourages his new couch purchase, saying, "People go over budget on movies every day! Why can't you go over budget on a couch?" Frank high-fives him. Paige begins to chastise Frank near the end of Day 2 for his wanton spending, and he explains that he had to buy everything for the room because it was empty. He laments, "What can you do with a box and a magazine rack? I mean, even Vern, my God, even Vern couldn't do anything with that!"

Designer Favorites

Frank says the Reveal of this room was most memorable for him, because, according to the homeowner, it was the first time he ever got what he asked for. Frank also says, "It was also a plus being around his [the homeowner's] remarkable photography."

Tough Talk

At the end of Designer Chat, Gen looks into the camera and warns, "You better love this, Robin. You better love this." Gen doesn't have to worry. The female homeowner, Robin, adores the room.

S3	
E51	

California: Via Jardin

💧 ✳ $ | **Cast:** Paige, Laurie, Vern, Amy Wynn | **Laurie's Room:** ☺ 😐 ☹ | **Vern's Room:** ☺ 😐 ☹

after

before

DESIGNED BY LAURIE

Budget Buster

In the end, Laurie is over by $31, and Vern is over by $1.94.

The
Rooms

Laurie warms up a living room by painting the walls orange, painting large bookshelves with black and red lacquer, building a vertical fireplace extension with an octagon motif made from decorative molding, creating a bamboo-framed full-length mirror, slipcovering the furniture with white fabric, and accenting a long wall with a row of white vertical rectangles made from molding. Vern softens the colors in a kitchen by painting the "slaughterhouse red" walls yellow-cream, expanding the island top, designing a seating bench with inside storage, turning a tall bookcase on its side to become a bench/shoe storage area, hanging stainless-steel pot shelving above the stove, and laying new wood laminate flooring.

Down and Out
Vern removes the existing ceiling fan and replaces it with a chandelier.

after

before

DESIGNED BY VERN

Deadly Design
Paige and Vern's female homeowner joke about Vern's storage bench design and think it could double as a casket. They even pretend to be kids who have to spend time in Vern's "time-out coffin."

Monumental Task
Vern reveals his plans to lay a laminate floor in the large kitchen, and Paige turns to the homeowners and deadpans, "Oh by the way, you're gonna be up all night and it's gonna be a lot of work. Welcome to *Trading Spaces*. Vern Yip is your designer."

Tearjerker
Upon seeing their rooms, both female homeowners cry tears of joy. The male kitchen homeowner tells Paige that his wife "didn't cry this much when [they] got married."

S3
E52

Los Angeles, CA: Seventh Street

★ ◊ $ | **Cast:** Paige, Edward, Hildi, Amy Wynn | Edward's Room: ☺ ☺ ☹ | Hildi's Room: ☺ ☺ ☹

The Rooms

after

Edward gets funky in Beverly Mitchell's garage rec room by painting the walls gray; building room screens that are painted gray and chartreuse; upholstering thrift store and existing furniture with chartreuse fabric; building a bar area; hanging white, gray, and chartreuse curtains on rods made of bent pipe to hide the laundry area; and hanging paper lanterns over the seating area. Hildi brings a little refinement to George and Jeff Stoltz's bachelor pad living room by covering the walls with blue faux suede, laying a khaki carpet, building a large armoire with woven raffia doors, installing a small wall near the front door to create a short hallway, reupholstering two thrift store sofas, building a small bar-style table, hanging a bike spray painted silver on the wall as sculpture, and framing black-and-white photos of Hildi's and her team's tummies.

DESIGNED BY EDWARD

before

Reveal-ing Moments

Jeff is silent for a long time after opening his eyes. Paige is concerned he's upset, but he finally says, "I wanted to come in and pretend like I was [upset] but I couldn't!" When she asks if they're ready to go see the girls' reaction to Beverly's room, Jeff asks, "Who cares?" and says that he wants to stay in his new room. Upon opening her eyes, Beverly cries happy tears and says, "Now I feel bad for calling [Jeff and George] slackers!"

Star Struck

The two sets of homeowners are stars of the TV show *Seventh Heaven:* Beverly Mitchell works with Jessica Biel, and brothers George and Jeff Stoltz make up the other team.

EDWARD R.I.P.

DESIGNED BY HILDI

REC · PAIGE CAM

Boys Will Be Boys

George and Jeff's living room is in horrible shape before Hildi cleans it up. There are piles of trash all around the room, and the floor is a cracked concrete slab. The boys confessed that their mother called, begging them to clean their bathroom before the *Trading Spaces* crew arrived. As the girls enter at the start of Day 1, Hildi exclaims, "Welcome to the fraternity!" Paige captures one of the boys' bedrooms on the PaigeCam and shows that the mattress is supported on milk crates filled with clothes. Beverly says, "We've got a good job. You can at least get a bed frame!" and Jessica mumbles, "That's gross."

after

before

Boys Will Be Boys 2

Beverly had forbidden the boys to sleep in her bedroom. Paige and Edward discover them there the morning of Day 2 with plates of sausages and dog food, Beverly's Nickelodeon Teen Choice award, and trash strewn all over her bed. They take several Polaroids of themselves doing things to mess up her bedroom that are eventually displayed in Edward's finished room.

Score!

Hildi and Jessica reupholster furniture on a balcony above the apartment building's pool. Hildi says that they're ditching the couch cushions and shows how serious she is by throwing them behind her into the pool. Jessica looks over the edge and says that they all made it into the water. Hildi asks how many points that is, and Jessica quickly says, "Forty. Ten each."

S3
E53

Orlando, FL: Winter Song Drive

⏣ ⬤ ✳ | **Cast:** Paige, Doug, Vern, Amy Wynn | **Doug's Room:** ☺ ☺ ☹ | **Vern's Room:** ☺ ☺ ☹

The Rooms

Doug gives an enclosed patio a martini bar look by painting the walls white, adding a marble tile top to an existing bar, covering the front of the bar with aluminum flashing, mounting a TV on the wall, hanging multiple white waterproof curtains, using silver conduit as a drapery rod, building banquette and upholstered cube seating, and attaching several round automotive mirrors to the wall. Vern gives new life to a living room by painting three walls taupe and one wall rust-red, laying a new seagrass rug, painting the existing armoire tan and the side tables rust-red, building an upholstered removable top for the coffee table so it can double as an ottoman, and buying a brown sectional sofa from a thrift store.

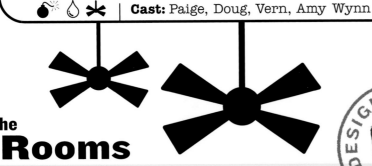
DESIGNED BY DOUG

Fan Philanthropy?
When Doug's homeowners ask him about the fate of the existing ceiling fan, he says, "It's gonna stay. I'm a giver." At the other house, Vern gives his homeowners the choice of leaving the existing ceiling fan or cutting it. They decide to get rid of it.

after

Bad Luck?
During both The Reveal and end credit shots of Designer Chat, Doug's automotive mirrors fall off the wall.

before

The Name Game: Doug (or Doogie, as Amy Wynn calls him in this episode) refers to his color scheme as **The Swedes Go to Southbeach.**

Eek!
In one scene Doug's relaxing in the outdoor hot tub while his homeowners hammer away in the background. He yells to them, "Shhh! I'm trying to plan!" Paige finds him and tells him to get out. Paige implies he's naked because as he starts to stand up, she looks down at him, screams, and looks away quickly saying, "Don't get out now!" He sits back down and asks her to refill his drink.

Doug and Amy Wynn pretend to be statues.

DESIGNED BY VERN

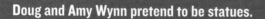

after

Uplifting Teamwork

Vern's male homeowner lifts Vern up and carries him out of the room at the start of Load Out. At the end of Day 2, Vern announces that they're done, and both of his homeowners carry him out on their shoulders.

Adhesive Neurosis

While applying squiggly lines of liquid adhesive to the back of a mirror, Vern confesses to his female homeowner, "This is driving me crazy right now that this isn't going on in a straight line."

Tearjerker: The female living room homeowner cries tears of joy.

By the Seat of His Pants

Vern and his team hop into the *Trading Spaces* pickup and drive to a thrift store to look for a sectional sofa to use in the room. Paige is in awe that he didn't pick it out before the show. Vern spends most of his budget ($600) on the chosen piece.

before

Demolition

Paige and Doug's female homeowner destroy the existing tiled bar top using hammers.

S3
E54

Orlando, FL: Whisper Lake

Cast: Paige, Frank, Hildi, Amy Wynn | Frank's Room: ☺ ☺ ☹ | Hildi's Room: ☺ ☺ ☹

The Rooms

Frank lightens a family room by dry-brushing the walls with white paint and the wainscoting with sage green paint, adding a broken tile mosaic to the existing fireplace, hanging fish netting as a valance, upholstering the existing furniture with sage green fabric, painting the existing armoire pale blue, and installing lighthouse-theme hardware on the armoire doors and drawers. Hildi spices up a living room by painting the walls brick red, slipcovering the furniture and making draperies from cream fabric printed with red Asian-themed designs, building a new wall to better define the space, demolishing a small half-wall, transforming wicker chicken cages into light fixtures, and painting the coffee and side tables brown.

after

before

Quotable Quotes

Frank-isms flow in this episode. On being under budget: "If [I'm] not, I could always lie. I'm not beneath that." To Amy Wynn: "My little wood nymph!" On how long his homeowners take to decide whether to paint or stain a portion of the wall: "I'm paralyzed with boredom." When Paige tells him, "This is a theme room to the nth degree," Frank replies, "And Orlando isn't?"

A Dream Is a Wish

During the Opener Paige stands in front of Cinderella's castle at Disney World. Hildi, Amy Wynn, and Frank are also at the Magic Kingdom, having their pictures taken with Pluto (Hildi's favorite Disney character) and Minnie Mouse. Paige calls Time's Up in her best Mickey Mouse voice as the famous mouse himself looks on.

Fan-tastic: Frank adds two white ceiling fans to his room. Hildi removes the existing fan in her room.

SHOCK VALUE

Hildi wants to demolish an existing half-wall, but Amy Wynn vetoes the idea because it's wired for an outlet and three light switches. Hildi doesn't take no for an answer, taking money out of her budget to hire an electrician to move the electrical components to another wall.

after

before

Feel the Love

Hildi's male homeowner leaves a note in his own home for Frank. On an 8x10 headshot he writes, "Frank, I love your work. I only hope I still do on Friday."

Amy Wynn Adoration

Hildi's male homeowner tells Amy Wynn, "I know a lot of women are probably disappointed that Ty isn't here, but on behalf of a lot of the men in America, I'm glad that you're here."

Budget Buster

Hildi's $11.87 over budget, while Frank's $105 over the spending limit. During Designer Chat he hands Paige a $100 bill, and she says that she'll spot him the extra five.

Congratulations!

The end credit shots are entirely of the cast and crew presenting Paige with a cake to celebrate her 100th episode on the show. She's overwhelmed with emotion and cries. Interestingly, this is the 100th episode she's taped, but at this point viewers have seen only 99. Tucson: Euclid was filmed during the third season but didn't air until the start of the fourth.

S3

E55

South Carolina: Innisbrook Lane

Cast: Paige, Frank, Laurie, Carter   Frank's Room: ☺ 😐 ☹ | Laurie's Room: ☺ 😐 ☹

The Rooms

Frank brightens a large living room by painting the walls yellow, decoupaging green and white marbled paper to insets on the fireplace, hanging navy blue drapes, slipcovering the furniture in both red and taupe fabric, laying a large natural-tone rug, and covering the bases of two new lamps with the same paper used on the fireplace. Laurie revamps a living room with a color palette inspired by a Van Gogh print. Three walls are painted sage green; the remaining wall is painted with horizontal stripes in sage green, olive green, yellow, and white; a new silver light fixture is hung; the furniture is rearranged into a more comfortable conversation area; doors are added to the existing armoire; and a large square fabric-topped coffee table is built complete with four large storage drawers.

after

before

Impressions, Anyone?

While talking with his female homeowner, Frank starts explaining his choice of yellow paint and concedes that it's a shade that Laurie uses often. He goes on to say in a soft voice, "She'd call it something like Amber Cream or Buttermilk Fawn. I just love the way she says, 'You know, I think this will be just perfect here, don't you?'"

Welcome!

This episode is Carter's _Trading Spaces_ debut.

Name Shame

While working on an art project, Frank asks Paige how to spell "Tracee," his female homeowner's name. Paige is suddenly shocked, saying, "It's Tracee?! Oh my gosh, I've been calling her Stacey the whole time!"

after

before

DESIGNED BY LAURIE

Getting in the Act

Paige is surrounded by *Trading Spaces* fans while filming the Opener in front of the two houses. The group of fans makes a reappearance near the end of the episode and calls Time's Up.

Fan Ban: Laurie removes the existing ceiling fan.

Tearjerker

The female green living room homeowner cries tears of joy. Both female homeowners cry happy tears when they come together at the end of The Reveals.

Age Matters

While building the storage drawers for Laurie's coffee table, Carter jokes with her male homeowner that he didn't have any toys when he was young. He says, "Back in the day, boy, we didn't have this kinda stuff." The homeowner jokingly asks, "What? Two or three years ago?"

Reveal-ing Moment

When Paige points out the storage in the coffee table to the male green living room homeowner, he says, "Who cares about the table? We got 10 lemons out of the deal," jokingly referring to a vase filled with lemons on top of the armoire. When Paige encourages him to feel the faux suede slipcover on the sofa he says, "I'm gonna get a jogging suit just like this!"

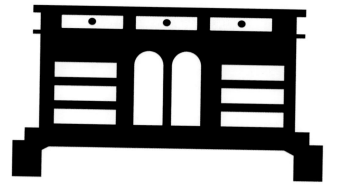

S3

E56

South Carolina: Sherborne Drive

✳ | **Cast:** Paige, Doug, Edward, Carter | **Doug's Room:** ☺ ☺ ☹ | **Edward's Room:** ☺ ☺ ☹

The Rooms

Doug creates a comfortable modern den by painting the walls dark plum-gray, laying a dark gray carpet, covering the ceiling with draped sheets of white poster board, installing a long L-shape banquette seating area with circular supports, building upholstered stools, hanging canvases and adding tufted pillows in light lavender shades, and creating a half-wall with strips of wood woven through pipe supports. Edward adds a modern twist to Moroccan style in a living room by painting the ceiling teal, texturing two of the walls with crumpled tissue paper, painting the walls mustard yellow, covering the brick fireplace with terra-cotta-tinted cement, building a large mantel spray-painted to look like stone, and adding wrought-iron decorative accents.

after

before

DESIGNED BY DOUG

Do You Really?
When Doug shows Paige his poster board ceiling she says, "It's a dust trap!" He explains that it's like a false ceiling so that dust will collect on it, but it won't be seen. He asks her, "Do you open up your false ceilings and dust them?" She replies, "Of course I do!"

Root for the Home Team
The cast wears baseball jerseys that read *Trading Spaces* during B-Roll footage and plays around at a ball field. Paige catches a ball in the outfield, Edward pitches, Doug bats, and Carter catches.

Um, Okay
Edward's homeowners present him with an unusual fish-shape water pitcher they want to have displayed in the room. It's on the mantel for The Reveal.

Reveal-ing Moment
When the four homeowners come together in the end, the female Modern Moroccan homeowner asks the female recipient of Doug's dark gray den, "What did you think of your place?" Her neighbor quickly responds, "I forgive you."

after

before

EDWARD

Down and Out: Doug removes the existing ceiling fan.

Pennsylvania: Tremont Drive

S3
E57

💧 $ | **Cast:** Paige, Genevieve, Vern, Amy Wynn | Genevieve's Room: ☺ 😐 ☹ | Vern's Room: ☺ 😐 ☹

after

before

DESIGNED BY GENEVIEVE

Tearjerker
Upon seeing her son's new bedroom, the female homeowner cries. Her son is overjoyed and repeatedly exclaims, "I love it!"

The Rooms

Gen kick-starts a boy's bedroom by painting the walls bright green, adding a black and white racing stripe around the room on the center of the walls, building a raised platform for the bed and desk, creating a seating area with a green rug and orange chairs, suspending several green and white paper lanterns above the bed, and adding multiple pieces of hockey memorabilia around the room. Vern designs an inviting living room by painting the walls gold, applying copper leaf to a large inset in the ceiling, slipcovering an existing and a thrift store sofa in brown velvet, building a chaise lounge, tiling the top of the existing coffee table with brown and gold glass tiles, and creating a large burgundy cabinet/bar wall unit by mixing ready-made and newly constructed pieces.

He Can't Even Defend Himself

While Amy Wynn builds Gen's bed platform, Gen sighs, "*Trading Spaces,* where everything seems to go wrong." Amy Wynn kids back, "That's because you have Ty working for you too often!"

after

before

DESIGNED BY VERN

Gender Wars
While using a nail gun with Amy Wynn, Vern's male homeowner says, "This is a man tool." Amy Wynn replies, "Um, excuse me?" The homeowner realizes his mistake and says, "I'm sorry. A Wynn tool." She points out, "It can't be a man tool if a woman has to show a man how to do it."

Budget Buster
Gen's signed hockey memorabilia puts her $10 over the $1,000 budget.

S3
E58

Pennsylvania: Bryant Court

? $ | **Cast:** Paige, Hildi, Laurie, Amy Wynn | Hildi's Room: ☺ ☺ ☹ | Laurie's Room: ☺ ☺ ☹

DESIGNED BY HILDI

The Rooms

Hildi makes a bold statement in a dining room by painting the walls and ceiling black, painting a thrift store table and chairs bright yellow, making a large black light fixture that holds 53 exposed light bulbs, hanging cream draperies, upholstering the dining chairs with twig-print cream fabric, hanging metal screens spray-painted chrome on the wall, and creating several flower arrangements in vases filled with boiled eggs. Laurie pumps up the pizzazz in a room shared by two little girls by painting the walls bright green, hand-painting large pink and yellow zinnias across the walls, building square headboards upholstered in pink and yellow plaid fabric, creating two new toy boxes painted with the girls' initials, painting the existing furniture and trim yellow, and creating a small tea table area.

after

before

Reveal-ing Moment

After seeing the black dining room, the male homeowner says, "I don't think it's that bad." His wife quickly replies, "I don't think it's that good."

Questionable Colors

Despite Hildi's confidence in her color choice, her homeowners aren't sure they like the overall design. Hildi's male homeowner describes the dining room's design to Amy Wynn by saying, "It's gonna be like a death room." Hildi's female homeowner refers to the yellow oval table as a "big egg yolk."

It's Not That Bad

Laurie's male homeowner wears a black T-shirt that reads, "Who's idea was this, anyway?" under his *Trading Spaces* smock. He later refers to the show as Trading Nightmares. Laurie tells her female homeowner that the show is "a game of risk and jeopardy."

after

DESIGNED BY LAURIE

before

Budget Buster

Both Laurie and Hildi are over budget in this episode: Laurie's final total is $1,001.07, and Hildi's is $1,026.00.

The Name Game: Laurie names her room Zany for Zinnias.

S3
E59

Pennsylvania: Cresheim Road

✳ $ | **Cast:** Paige, Hildi, Kia, Amy Wynn | Hildi's Room: ☺ ☺ ☹ | Kia's Room: ☺ ☺ ☹

after

The Rooms

Hildi goes glam in an office by painting the walls and trim magenta, laying black foam squares as carpeting, building an 11-foot-long couch upholstered in pink python-print vinyl with white lights underneath, sewing purple sequined throw pillows, hanging magenta velvet drapes, building a large white desk unit, and adding a magenta chair. Kia gets musical in a kitchen by painting the walls "turmeric yellow," painting the trim white, installing a sheet-metal backsplash, adding new cabinets and countertops, decoupaging sheet music on the top of a new island, suspending a trombone to be used as a pot rack, and creating a cabinet door that looks like a large bass complete with vintage accessories.

before

You Don't Say!
Hildi tells her team about one of her purchases for the room, saying, "I found these lights that, you know, light up."

The Name Game: Hildi names her room Mom's Lipstick Palace.

Budget Buster
Kia's musical instrument pieces put her $79 over budget. She cheerfully tells Paige, "That's better than $100!"

Presto Change-O
Kia removes a rectangular fluorescent light fixture and replaces it with a ceiling fan.

after

The Morning After
Kia arrives the morning of Day 2 to find her homeowners sitting outside barefoot and wearing robes. They tell her they've had a hard time getting moving. Hildi arrives and finds her team sitting outside with an old, large picture of one of their neighbors in a tux serving drinks and say that they're using the shot to inspire them throughout the day.

before

Designer Favorites
Kia says this is one of her favorite rooms she's designed for the show.

" **Green team rules, red team drools!** "

—Kia's team teases its neighbors after the Key Swap

Index

The Hosts
Alex: Appeared in Season I (40 episodes)
Paige: Appeared in Seasons 2 and 3 (I04 episodes)

The Designers
Dez: Appeared in Season I (5 episodes)
Doug: Appeared in Seasons I–3 (45 episodes)
Edward: Appeared in Season 3 (9 episodes)
Frank: Appeared in Seasons I–3 (47 episodes)
Genevieve: Appeared in Seasons I–3 (46 episodes)
Hildi: Appeared in Seasons I–3 (47 episodes)
Kia: Appeared in Season 3 (I0 episodes)
Laurie: Appeared in Seasons I–3 (40 episodes)
Roderick: Appeared in Season I (I episode)
Vern: Appeared in Seasons I–3 (38 episodes)

The Carpenters
Amy Wynn: Appeared in Seasons I–3 (72 episodes)
Carter: Appeared in Season 3 (2 episodes)
Handy Andy: Appeared in Season 3 (I episode)
Ty: Appeared in Seasons I–3 (69 episodes)

The Rooms
Basement/Recreational Room
Doug: Washington, D.C.: Cleveland Park (SI, E7)
Genevieve: Philadelphia, PA: Galahad Road (SI, EI2)
Frank: Knoxville, TN: Courtney Oak (SI, EI3)
Frank: Knoxville, TN: Stubbs Bluff (SI, E20)
Hildi: Quakertown, PA: Quakers Way (S2, EI)
Laurie: New Jersey: Tall Pines Drive (S2, E2)
Genevieve: Philadelphia, PA: Jeannes Street (S2, EI0)
Genevieve: Chicago, IL: Fairview Avenue (S2, EI6)
Hildi: Seattle, WA: 56th Place (S2, E23)
Laurie: Los Angeles, CA: Springdale Drive (S2, E34)
Kia: New York: Half Hollow Turn (S3, E7)

Bathroom
Hildi: Mississippi: Golden Pond (S3, E27)

Bedroom (Adult)
Doug: Knoxville, TN: Forest Glen (SI, E2)
Laurie: Knoxville, TN: Courtney Oak (SI, EI3)
Laurie: Cincinnati, OH: Madison & Forest (SI, EI6)
Genevieve: San Diego, CA: Elm Ridge (SI, EI7)
Hildi: San Diego, CA: Elm Ridge (SI, EI7)
Dez: Miami, FL: I68th/83rd Streets (SI, E2I)
Hildi: Orlando, FL: Lake Catherine (SI, E27)
Genevieve: Orlando, FL: Gotha Furlong (SI, E28)
Frank: Orlando, FL: Gotha Furlong (SI, E28)
Genevieve: New Orleans, LA: Walter Road (SI, E33)
Vern: New York: Sherwood Drive (SI, E36)
Doug: New York: Sherwood Drive (SI, E36)
Hildi: New Jersey: Sam Street (SI, E38)
Vern: New Jersey: Tall Pines Drive (S2, E2)
Laurie: Maple Glen, PA: Fiedler Road (S2, E3)
Genevieve: Providence, RI: Wallis Avenue (S2, E6)
Doug: Boston, MA: Institute Road (S2, E9)
Laurie: New Jersey: Perth Road (S2, EII)
Genevieve: Maryland: Village Green (S2, EI2)
Doug: Maryland: Village Green (S2, EI2)
Vern: Maryland: Fairway Court (S2, EI3)

Doug: Maryland: Fairway Court (S2, EI3)
Hildi: Chicago, IL: Spaulding Avenue (S2, EI5)
Frank: Colorado: Stoneflower Drive (S2, E20)
Laurie: Seattle, WA: Dakota Street (S2, E22)
Hildi: Oregon: Alyssum Avenue (S2, E24)
Vern: California: Corte Rosa (S2, E28)
Laurie: California: Corte Rosa (S2, E28)
Vern: California: Grenadine Way (S2, E29)
Genevieve: Texas: Sherwood Street (S2, E37)
Doug: Houston, TX: Appalachian Trail (S2, E39)
Hildi: Plano, TX: Shady Valley Road (S2, E4I)
Hildi: Raleigh, NC: Legging Lane (S2, E43)
Doug: North Carolina: Southerby Drive (S2, E44)
Hildi: North Carolina: Southerby Drive (S2, E44)
Vern: Wake Forest, NC: Rodney Bay (S2, E45)
Laurie: Maine: Joseph Drive (S3, E3)
Frank: Maine: Joseph Drive (S3, E3)
Edward: Long Island, NY: Steuben Boulevard (S3, E4)
Genevieve: New York: Whitlock Road (S3, E6)
Doug: New York: Whitlock Road (S3, E6)
Genevieve: Philadelphia, PA: 22nd Street (S3, E8)
Frank: Pennsylvania: Gorski Lane (S3, EI0)
Doug: Pennsylvania: Gorski Lane (S3, EI0)
Edward: Long Island, NY: Dover Court (S3, EII)
Hildi: New Jersey: Catania Court (S3, EI5)
Kia: Virginia: Gentle Heights Court (S3, EI7)
Hildi: Arlington, VA: First Road (S3, EI8)
Doug: Arlington, VA: First Road (S3, EI8)
Vern: Washington, D.C.: Quebec Place (S3, EI9)
Doug: Indiana: Fieldhurst Lane (S3, E2I)
Vern: Indiana: Fieldhurst Lane (S3, E2I)
Edward: Indiana: Halleck Way (S3, E22)
Kia: Indiana: Halleck Way (S3, E22)
Genevieve: Missouri: Sunburst Drive (S3, E23)
Vern: Missouri: Sunburst Drive (S3, E23)
Edward: Missouri: Sweetbriar Lane (S3, E25)
Frank: Missouri: Sweetbriar Lane (S3, E25)
Genevieve: London: Garden Flat (S3, E26)
Laurie: Mississippi: Golden Pond (S3, E27)
Laurie: Mississippi: Winsmere Way (S3, E28)
Hildi: Mississippi: Winsmere Way (S3, E28)
Genevieve: San Clemente, CA: Camino Mojada (S3, E33)
Doug: California: Dusty Trail (S3, E34)
Frank: California: Fairfield (S3, E35)
Frank: San Diego, CA: Duenda Road (S3, E36)
Vern: Scottsdale, AZ: Bell Road (S3, E38)
Doug: Scottsdale, AZ: Windrose Avenue (S3, E39)
Frank: Scottsdale, AZ: Windrose Avenue (S3, E39)
Doug: Vegas, NV: Carlsbad Caverns (S3, E40)
Kia: Miami, FL: Ten Court (S3, E43)
Frank: Miramar, FL: Avenue I64 (S3, E45)
Kia: Orlando, FL: Smith Street (S3, E46)
Edward: Florida: Night Owl Lane (S3, E47)
Vern: Santa Monica, CA: Ocean Park (S3, E49)

Bedroom (Children's)
Frank: Athens, GA: County Road (SI, E3)
Genevieve: Cincinnati, OH: Sturbridge Road (SI, EI5)
Doug: Orlando, FL: Winterhaven (SI, E29)

Vern: New Orleans, LA: D'evereaux Street (SI, E34)
Laurie: Boston, MA: Ashfield Street (S2, E7)
Genevieve: Boston, MA: Ashfield Street (S2, E7)
Vern: Long Island, NY: Dover Court (S3, EII)
Hildi: Virginia: Gentle Heights Court (S3, EI7)
Doug: Scott Air Force Base, MO: Ash Creek (S3, E24)
Hildi: London: Garden Flat (S3, E26)
Frank: Scottsdale, AZ: Bell Road (S3, E38)
Genevieve: Pennsylvania: Tremont Drive (S3, E57)
Laurie: Pennsylvania: Bryant Court (S3, E58)

Bonus Room
Vern: Austin, TX: La Costa Drive (S2, E36)

Chapter Room (Fraternity and Sorority)
Laurie (sorority): Santa Clara, CA: Lafayette Street (S2, E27)
Doug (fraternity): Berkeley, CA: Prospect Street (S2, E30)
Genevieve (sorority): Berkeley, CA: Prospect Street (S2, E30)

Den
Frank: Knoxville, TN: Fourth & Gill (SI, EI)
Doug: South Carolina: Sherborne Drive (S3, E56)

Dining Room
Hildi: Alpharetta, GA: Providence Oaks (SI, E4)
Laurie: Philadelphia, PA: Valley Road (SI, EII)
Doug: Cincinnati, OH: Sturbridge Road (SI, EI5)
Hildi: Austin, TX: Wycliff (SI, E24)
Laurie: New Jersey: Sam Street (SI, E38)
Doug: California: Peralta Street (S2, E32)
Vern: Los Angeles, CA: Springdale Drive (S2, E34)
Frank: Long Island, NY: Steuben Boulevard (S3, E4)
Genevieve: New Jersey: Catania Court (S3, EI5)
Laurie: Austin, TX: Wyoming Valley Drive (S3, E30)
Hildi: Pennsylvania: Bryant Court (S3, E58)

Family Room
Doug: Portland, OR: Everett Street (S2, E26)
Frank: Orlando, FL: Whisper Lake (S3, E54)

Garage Recreational Room
Edward: Los Angeles, CA: Seventh Street (S3, E52)

Guest Bedroom
Kia: Pennsylvania: Victoria Drive (S3, EI2)

Kitchen
Laurie: Knoxville, TN: Fourth & Gill (SI, EI)
Genevieve: Buckhead, GA: Canter Road (SI, E6)
Frank: Alexandria, VA: Riefton Court (SI, E8)
Laurie: Annapolis, MD: Fox Hollow (SI, E9)
Hildi: Cincinnati, OH: Melrose Avenue (SI, EI4)
Laurie: San Diego, CA: Hermes Avenue (SI, EI8)
Doug: San Diego, CA: Wilbur Street (SI, EI9)
Doug: Knoxville, TN: Stubbs Bluff (SI, E20)
Hildi: Fort Lauderdale, FL: 59th Street (SI, E22)
Doug: Austin, TX: Wycliff (SI, E24)
Genevieve: Austin, TX: Wing Road (SI, E25)
Vern: Orlando, FL: Lake Catherine (SI, E27)
Vern: Santa Fe, NM: Felize (SI, E3I)
Hildi: New Orleans, LA: Jacob Street (SI, E32)
Frank: New Orleans, LA: Walter Road (SI, E33)

Laurie: New Jersey: Lincroft (S1, E39)
Frank: Providence, RI: Wallis Avenue (S2, E6)
Frank: Chicago, IL: Edward Road (S2, E14)
Vern: Chicago, IL: Fairview Avenue (S2, E16)
Genevieve: Colorado: Berry Avenue (S2, E17)
Frank: Oregon: Alsea Court (S2, E25)
Genevieve: Oakland, CA: Webster Street (S2, E31)
Frank: Texas: Sherwood Street (S2, E37)
Laurie: Texas: Sutton Court (S2, E42)
Doug: Maine: George Road (S3, E1)
Genevieve: Maine: George Road (S3, E1)
Genevieve: Long Island, NY: Split Rock Road (S3, E5)
Vern: Long Island, NY: Split Rock Road (S3, E5)
Frank: Philadelphia, PA: Gettysburg Lane (S3, E9)
Doug: Nazareth, PA: First Street (S3, E14)
Hildi: Austin, TX: Wyoming Valley Drive (S3, E30)
Genevieve: California: Dusty Trail (S3, E34)
Doug: Miramar, FL: Avenue 164 (S3, E45)
Vern: California: Via Jardin (S3, E51)
Kia: Pennsylvania: Cresheim Road (S3, E59)

Library
Frank: Boston, MA: Institute Road (S2, E9)

Living Room
Hildi: Knoxville, TN: Forest Glen (S1, E2)
Dez: Lawrenceville, GA: Pine Lane (S1, E5)
Hildi: Lawrenceville, GA: Pine Lane (S1, E5)
Laurie: Buckhead, GA: Canter Road (S1, E6)
Dez: Washington, D.C.: Cleveland Park (S1, E7)
Genevieve: Alexandria, VA: Riefton Court (S1, E8)
Genevieve: Annapolis, MD: Fox Hollow (S1, E9)
Frank: Philadelphia, PA: Strathmore Road (S1, E10)
Dez: Philadelphia, PA: Strathmore Road (S1, E10)
Frank: Cincinnati, OH: Melrose Avenue (S1, E14)
Doug: Cincinnati, OH: Madison & Forest (S1, E16)
Genevieve: San Diego, CA: Hermes Avenue (S1, E18)
Frank: San Diego, CA: Wilbur Street (S1, E19)
Laurie: Miami, FL: 168th/83rd Streets (S1, E21)
Frank: Fort Lauderdale, FL: 59th Street (S1, E22)
Frank: Key West, FL: Elizabeth Street (S1, E23)
Genevieve: Key West, FL: Elizabeth Street (S1, E23)
Hildi: Austin, TX: Wing Road (S1, E25)
Frank: Austin, TX: Birdhouse Drive (S1, E26)
Laurie: Orlando, FL: Winterhaven (S1, E29)
Hildi: Albuquerque, NM: Gloria (S1, E30)
Doug: Albuquerque, NM: Gloria (S1, E30)
Genevieve: Santa Fe, NM: Felize (S1, E31)
Dez: New York: Shore Road (S1, E35)
Doug: New York: Linda Court (S1, E37)
Frank: New York: Linda Court (S1, E37)
Doug: New Jersey: Lincroft (S1, E39)
Vern: New Jersey: Lafayette Street (S1, E40)
Doug: Quakertown, PA: Quakers Way (S2, E1)
Genevieve: Maple Glen, PA: Fiedler Road (S2, E3)
Hildi: Northampton, PA: James Avenue (S2, E4)
Frank: Northampton, PA: James Avenue (S2, E4)
Hildi: Providence, RI: Phillips Street (S2, E5)
Vern: Providence, RI: Phillips Street (S2, E5)
Hildi: Springfield, MA: Sunset Terrace (S2, E8)
Vern: Springfield, MA: Sunset Terrace (S2, E8)
Vern: Philadelphia, PA: Jeannes Street (S2, E10)
Frank: New Jersey: Perth Road (S2, E11)
Laurie: Chicago, IL: Edward Road (S2, E14)
Doug: Chicago, IL: Spaulding Avenue (S2, E15)
Hildi: Colorado: Berry Avenue (S2, E17)

Genevieve: Colorado: Cherry Street (S2, E18)
Laurie: Colorado: Cherry Street (S2, E18)
Frank: Colorado: Andes Way (S2, E19)
Vern: Colorado: Andes Way (S2, E19)
Doug: Colorado: Stoneflower Drive (S2, E20)
Doug: Seattle, WA: 137th Street (S2, E21)
Frank: Seattle, WA: 137th Street (S2, E21)
Vern: Seattle, WA: Dakota Street (S2, E22)
Genevieve: Seattle, WA: 56th Place (S2, E23)
Genevieve: Oregon: Alyssum Avenue (S2, E24)
Laurie: Oregon: Alsea Court (S2, E25)
Frank: Santa Clara, CA: Lafayette Street (S2, E27)
Frank: California: Grenadine Way (S2, E29)
Hildi: Oakland, CA: Webster Street (S2, E31)
Hildi: California: Peralta Street (S2, E32)
Doug: Los Angeles, CA: Willoughby Avenue (S2, E33)
Genevieve: Los Angeles, CA: Willoughby Avenue (S2, E33)
Frank: California: Abbeywood Lane (S2, E35)
Hildi: California: Abbeywood Lane (S2, E35)
Laurie: Houston, TX: Sawdust Street (S2, E38)
Doug: Houston, TX: Sawdust Street (S2, E38)
Vern: Plano, TX: Bent Horn Court (S2, E40)
Frank: Texas: Sutton Court (S2, E42)
Laurie: Wake Forest, NC: Rodney Bay (S2, E45)
Laurie: Portland, OR: Rosemont Avenue (S3, E2)
Vern: Portland, OR: Rosemont Avenue (S3, E2)
Frank: New York: Half Hollow Turn (S3, E7)
Edward: Philadelphia, PA: 22nd Street (S3, E8)
Vern: Philadelphia, PA: Gettysburg Lane (S3, E9)
Doug: Pennsylvania: Victoria Drive (S3, E12)
Doug: New Jersey: Manitoba Trail (S3, E13)
Vern: Nazareth, PA: First Street (S3, E14)
Hildi: Philadelphia, PA: East Avenue (S3, E16)
Frank: Philadelphia, PA: East Avenue (S3, E16)
Genevieve: Washington, D.C.: Quebec Place (S3, E19)
Genevieve: Indiana: River Valley Drive (S3, E20)
Doug: Indiana: River Valley Drive (S3, E20)
Hildi: San Antonio, TX: Ghostbridge (S3, E29)
Vern: San Antonio, TX: Ghostbridge (S3, E29)
Frank: Austin, TX: Aire Libre Drive (S3, E31)
Kia: Austin, TX: Aire Libre Drive (S3, E31)
Genevieve: Austin, TX: Wampton Way (S3, E32)
Doug: Austin, TX: Wampton Way (S3, E32)
Vern: San Diego, CA: Duenda Road (S3, E36)
Laurie: Los Angeles, CA: Murietta Avenue (S3, E37)
Hildi: Vegas, NV: Carlsbad Caverns (S3, E40)
Laurie: Vegas, NV: Smokemont Courts (S3, E41)
Genevieve: Vegas, NV: Woodmore Court (S3, E42)
Vern: Vegas, NV: Woodmore Court (S3, E42)
Hildi: Miami, FL: Ten Court (S3, E43)
Hildi: Miami, FL: Miami Place (S3, E44)
Laurie: Miami, FL: Miami Place (S3, E44)
Hildi: Florida: Night Owl Lane (S3, E47)
Laurie: Santa Monica, CA: Ocean Park (S3, E49)
Frank: Los Angeles, CA: Irving Street (S3, E50)
Genevieve: Los Angeles, CA: Irving Street (S3, E50)
Laurie: California: Via Jardin (S3, E51)
Hildi: Los Angeles, CA: Seventh Street (S3, E52)
Vern: Orlando, FL: Winter Song Drive (S3, E53)
Hildi: Orlando, FL: Whisper Lake (S3, E54)
Frank: South Carolina: Innisbrook Lane (S3, E55)
Laurie: South Carolina: Innisbrook Lane (S3, E55)
Edward: South Carolina: Sherborne Drive (S3, E56)
Vern: Pennsylvania: Tremont Drive (S3, E57)

Multipurpose Room
Hildi (kitchen/living room):
    Athens, GA: County Road (S1, E3)
Roderick (den/guest room):
    Alpharetta, GA: Providence Oaks (S1, E4)
Hildi (living/dining room):
    Philadelphia, PA: Galahad Road (S1, E12)
Laurie (living/dining room):
    Austin, TX: Birdhouse Drive (S1, E26)
Laurie (kitchen/office/dining/living room):
    New Orleans, LA: Jacob Street (S1, E32)
Genevieve (den/guest room):
    New Orleans, LA: D'evereaux Street (S1, E34)
Frank (dining/living room):
    New Jersey: Lafayette Street (S1, E40)
Vern (living/dining room):
    Portland, OR: Everett Street (S2, E26)
Laurie (office/playroom):
    Houston, TX: Appalachian Trail (S2, E39)
Frank (living/dining room):
    New Jersey: Manitoba Trail (S3, E13)
Kia (living/dining room):
    Scott Air Force Base, MO: Ash Creek (S3, E24)
Kia (office/game room):
    California: Fairfield (S3, E35)
Genevieve (living/dining room):
    Los Angeles, CA: Murietta Avenue (S3, E37)
Hildi (bedroom/dining room/entertaining area/office):
    Orlando, FL: Smith Street (S3, E46)
Vern (kitchen/breakfast nook):
    Los Angeles, CA: Elm Street (S3, E48)

Office
Edward: Vegas, NV: Smokemont Courts (S3, E41)
Genevieve: Los Angeles, CA: Elm Street (S3, E48)
Hildi: Pennsylvania: Cresheim Road (S3, E59)

Patio
Doug: Orlando, FL: Winter Song Drive (S3, E53)

Playroom
Genevieve: Plano, TX: Bent Horn Court (S2, E40)
Doug: Plano, TX: Shady Valley Road (S2, E41)
Frank: Raleigh, NC: Legging Lane (S2, E43)

Sewing Room
Hildi: Austin, TX: La Costa Drive (S2, E36)

Sunporch/Sun Room
Doug: Philadelphia, PA: Valley Road (S1, E11)
Genevieve: New York: Shore Road (S1, E35)

TV Room
Vern: San Clemente, CA: Camino Mojada (S3, E33)

Bring Trading Spaces to your home.

AVAILABLE NOW!

COMING SOON!

Decorate the Trading Spaces way with books based on the hit TV show.

You'll **learn techniques** and **gain confidence** to redo a room **like the pros.**

SPRING 2004!
Trading Spaces 48-Hour Makeovers
Trading Spaces $100 to $1000 Makeovers